COULD I VOTE DA?

COULD I VOTE DA?

A Voter's Dilemma

Eusebius McKaiser

BOOK**STORM**

ISBN: 978-1-920434-55-7
e-ISBN: 978-1-920434-56-4

First edition, first impression 2014

Published by Bookstorm (Pty) Ltd
PO Box 4532
Northcliff 2115
Johannesburg
South Africa
www.bookstorm.co.za

Distributed by On the Dot
www.onthedot.co.za

Edited by Sharon Dell
Proofread by Sean Fraser
Cover design by mr design
Book design and typesetting by Triple M Design
Printed by Ultra Litho (Pty) Ltd, Johannesburg

CONTENTS

INTRODUCTION

Confessions of a confused voter

On the 18th of May 2011, I woke up to a beautiful autumn morning in my flat in bohemian Melville, Johannesburg. It was quiet outside; no trace of Mandela's born-free generation who revel here at night-time. There was another reason, however, for this particular day's early-morning tranquility. It was a public holiday, and that's always reason for self-declared overworked South Africans to sleep in before turning their attention to the braai. Or, at least, that was my fear. 'Fear' because the public holiday was actually the occasion of the local government election. Commentators had pretended to be sangomas with predictive powers, and many asserted that voter turnout would be low. As I left my apartment to go and vote in Sandton (where I had lived before), the silence that enveloped me outside seemed to vindicate the sceptics. But, it was still early.

As it happened, it was a hugely successful election from a voter turnout perspective – some 57.6% of registered voters cast their ballots, in enviable contrast to many democracies around the world that often have local election voter turnouts below 40%. So much for the assumption that dissatisfaction with service delivery would lead to black African voters in particular staying away from the polls in non-violent protest.

I was up early because I *had* to vote early. I was due to cover the elections for a television station as one of its rotating studio anchors, so would not have time to stand in a voting queue later. As the cab made its way from Melville through Parktown North, Rosebank, and from there to Sandton via Illovo, a single thought preoccupied my 32-year-old head. Who should I vote for, I wondered? I had still not made up my mind. I had two votes up for grabs, one for the proportional representation candidate from a party in whose ideas I had faith, and one for a directly elected ward candidate (on the basis of the first-past-the-post yardstick). I had no clue who to vote for. *No* clue.

For years I found the basic policy positions of the African National Congress (ANC) compelling. The party supports the idea of a welfare state, which I am grateful for as a first-generation black graduate who inherited the burden of having to send remittances home to poor family members. I have seen poverty. I have experienced it. And I have, more importantly, witnessed the social context in which poor people's agency remains undeveloped. A tough-love approach to poverty just does not sit well with me emotionally. My underperforming siblings did not choose, in any straightforward sense of the word, to drop out of school, and to have teen pregnancies. So I am grateful that a social security system is in place to ensure their kids don't starve during a month that Uncle Eusebius is unable to top them up. The ANC gets this.

And, in addition, the ANC understood very quickly after democracy's birth that the world is governed by a neo-liberal economic framework. The principles of neo-liberal economics are many and complex. The basic philosophical change the ANC had to make – and did (in no small part due to the hard work of that famous Aids denialist but reasonably gifted economics graduate, one Thabo Mbeki) – was to let go of socialist-inspired ideas of heavy state involvement in the economy and to accept that markets are fairly efficient mechanisms for allocating resources, determining where 'supply and demand' should settle, what wage levels are economically sustainable, etc. In practical terms, this meant abandoning policies like the Reconstruction and Development Programme (RDP), and settling for investment-friendly, growth-conducive policies that would hopefully still generate jobs.

Of course, many left-leaning economists will remind us of the jobless growth years during Mbeki's time in office. The point simply is that one would be unkind and frankly wrong to characterise the ANC as failing to choose a macroeconomic framework consistent with a world in which market-based economic activity had won the ideological battle against communist, command-based systems.

And, when it comes to social policies to do with lifestyle and identity issues, I was happy with the ANC too. Of course there are homophobes and sexist pigs in the ANC. That has to be the case in any big party that attracts members and supporters from across society. And yet the ANC leadership (or most of it) was happy to toe the liberal line *when it mattered*. The ANC, for example, gave their MPs no choice in 2006 but to vote in favour of the Civil Unions Bill which extended marriage rights to gay couples. They did not allow MPs to vote according to conscience, as the Democratic Alliance did in a fit of illiberalism.

The ANC placed a higher premium on substantive equality for gay and lesbian South Africans than on the personal beliefs about homosexuality that might be lurking in the hearts of MPs. The ANC, similarly, never used its parliamentary majority to undo very liberal positions on the death penalty, corporal punishment and other social issues that flowed from Constitutional Court judgments.

This is not to say I am overly grateful that the ANC is doing what it ought to do anyway, which is respect the standards that we as a society chose to be bound by legally and constitutionally. But as someone deeply committed to the ideal of a liberal society, I was comfortable with the ANC's nominal, if not always heartfelt, support of liberal social policies. The ANC ultimately accepts, even if sometimes grudgingly, that individual autonomy should not be sacrificed in the name of populism.

And so, as I was on my way to vote that morning, I found it tempting to reward the ANC for policies and ideologies that resonate deeply with my personal experiences, with my family's desperate situation back in Grahamstown, and with my commitment to liberalism.

And yet I wasn't sure I could actually get myself to vote for the ANC. Given how endemic corruption has become in the state under successive ANC governments, the gap between the policy ideals and delivery was (and still is) big and growing. Commentators' predictions of poor voter turnout weren't misplaced, even if they turned out to be false: the daily experiences of millions of South Africans remain that of being marginalised and effectively disenfranchised. Worse, there was (and is) an unsettling arrogance and political entitlement that too many ANC politicians and ANC-appointed government officials display.

I found myself wondering, 'Eusebius, do you really want to reward the arrogance of so many underperforming, ethically wayward ANC politicians? Do you?' I could not honestly answer in the affirmative. Not with a clear conscience, anyway. After all, as much as I enjoy policy and ideological debates, these are irrelevant if people's lives don't really change. Not to mention that by that time I had met and engaged plenty of tripartite alliance politicians whose gigantic egos and sense of entitlement had left a bad taste in my mouth.

For example, I once had to interview the ANC's Treasurer-General Mathews Phosa for SABC3's *Interface*. It was our first meeting. When I arrived for the pre-recording, he was already in the studio, having arrived earlier than scheduled. He had hardly greeted me before he started shouting at me for being late (which I was not), and then demanded to know, in the most sarcastic tone imaginable, whether I intended to apologise. He then advised me to do so. His entire demeanour during that tirade was that of someone who believed himself to be the king of the SABC. There was no appreciation of the fact that he was merely a guest on a current-affairs show that would give him the *privilege* of presenting his views to the public and to voters. Instead, he behaved as if he owned the place.

I am not easily taken aback by such behaviour. But I was then. For a brief second, I was even intimidated. What shocked me most was realising the casual silence of my colleagues who had been at the SABC for a long time. It dawned on me that the Phosas from the ANC are not only used to behaving as if the voter owes them something, they are also, and tragically so, used to engaging with many people within state-owned entities, like the SABC, who affirm this misplaced sense of political entitlement.

My fear gave way to anger and determination, and when the interview eventually started, I asked him particularly tough questions to see how well he could defend ANC policies and government performance.

He only relaxed his attitude once he realised that he was not dealing with a fearful stooge. By now my colleagues' jaws were on the floor, obviously not accustomed to a BBC Tim Sebastian-style of interviewing at the SABC.

To Phosa's great credit, however, I must add that once he accepted that I was doing my job and that I was insisting on doing my job honestly, we both thoroughly enjoyed the interview.

During one of the breaks he quipped, 'You are having great fun, aren't you?' And he smiled. I responded, with a dash of cheek, 'I am indeed! And you too, right?!' He left the studio after giving me a firm, friendly handshake.

But Phosa's initial outburst and arrogance are typical of the behaviour of many senior ANC leaders and government officials. Too many of them are not embarrassed either by their own underperformance or their tendency to drop the ethical ball. Even younger leaders, like former ANC Youth League spokesperson Floyd Shivambu, tend to mimic their political mentors and heroes. I have witnessed this. I have also encountered it myself on too many occasions.

These and other examples came to mind that morning of the 2011 local government elections. And I simply could not bring myself to commit to voting for a party with such characters.

I contemplated an alternative: vote, perhaps, for the Democratic Alliance (DA)?

But this thought also left me unsatisfied. On the one hand, there seemed to be decent evidence that where the DA runs municipalities, they do so quite effectively. DA councillors seem to have a good work ethic and a genuine desire to put grand ideological and policy squabbles aside and to simply get on with the practicalities of making communities safer, filling potholes, helping to sort out your billing problems, etc. Why would you not want a local government representative who will improve the quality of life you live in your part of the city? That seemed like a no-brainer – if you didn't give it any further thought.

As I was wondering whether to take a chance on the biggest opposition party, my cab happened to pass a golf course somewhere in the Parktown North area. And I found myself looking at luscious greens, greens that do not know what it is like to be obscured by the kind of litter that blocks drains in our townships and causes an overflow of unsafe water. The stuff in front of me was an aesthetic feast for hungry eyes.

I noticed a few men playing a round of golf, about five of them. And, not being colour-blind, I noticed that they were white, middle-aged, portly and having a jolly good time chuckling and exchanging banter. There were five other men with them, all of them black, and in charge of the white men's sports gear. They were, of course, the caddies. That picture made me feel funny, knotty thingies in my tummy. It reminded me of the lingering structural inequalities in South Africa that still make it more likely that a black person ends up being the *handlanger* (the help) and a white person ends up being *baas* (the boss).

The DA just does not get this stuff. Most DA supporters, and especially DA leaders, would react to this kind of experience dismissively. Some would rush to explain that whites simply enjoy golf more, just like blacks enjoy soccer more. So they'd criticise my visceral reaction as symptomatic of *me* having a racial problem. Others would be offended that I even told the story with reference to the skin colour of the two groups of men on that golf course. Why not, they might ask, simply refer to rich men and poor men? Isn't golf just an activity that correlates with wealth more so than with skin colour? Many black men who are wealthy now play golf, and surely poor white men on the outskirts of Pretoria would also feel out of place on the golf course? This is the kind of well-rehearsed pushback that I knew would roll off the tongue of a typical DA interlocutor. Or, at least, such has been my experience.

And, in a narrow academic sense, these are decent jabs. (I won't answer them here because responses are not salient to the overall point of the story.) The problem is that all of these clever little argumentation moves fail a very different test when it comes to politics: do you, as a politician, get the *heart* of the voter? Do you *feel* them? Do you recognise the history that explains why they see the world as they do? Do you even know, let alone care, how they see the world? And on this score, too many DA politicians, especially white ones (including the white liberals), simply do not *get* the black majority. They dismiss our racial identities and lived realities from an ahistoric, colour-blind platform.

Can I really vote for a party that reduces political life to an academic exercise in rational-choice theory? Can I trust this party to understand that my sisters are not self-made losers but two adults who were caught in a vicious cycle of intergenerational violence, poverty and neglect? I could not trust the DA to get this. My sisters, for DA policymakers, would be mere 'objects of social policy', as the English philosopher PF Strawson once said of mentally ill people.

I was not comfortable with the prospect of voting for a party that waspishly dismisses the emotional connections I have with my country's history, a history that reaches deep into the post-democracy. I was not comfortable voting for a party that laughs at me for refusing to reduce the voting process to a spreadsheet calculation filled with data points.

How could I vote for the DA then?

By now I had reached the queue at the Sandton Fire Station and was edging closer to the front. And still I had no clue. What a horrible choice: an incumbent political party that has a decent vision but which suffers from profound leadership and ethical crises? Or an opposition party filled with well-meaning, decently skilled, hardworking councillors with a tragically misplaced set of convictions about the impact of the past on the present, about where we are at currently, and about where we should be headed? South Africa, I realised, was a horrible place to be for a critically minded voter with a deep sense of history. Critical-mindedness will inevitably result in you rightly indicting an underperforming ANC. And yet a deep sense of history will leave you disappointed with the glib ahistoricism of too many leaders within the DA.

So, what to do? Split my vote, perhaps?

I only registered the answer after my hands and fingers had gone through the voting process and did the thinking for me. Perhaps, in the end, it was a random set of choices that I made. Political analysts are not immune to the vagaries of being human.

But my ultimate lack of control over that voting decision isn't my fault, I insist. I blame our two biggest political parties for leaving me a confused voter.

* * *

What has become clear to me since those elections, however, is that whichever party is in government, we will only ever have a sustainable and stable democracy if we have a competitive political system. This means that a ruling party, ideally, needs to harbour some fear that it might lose an election. Such fear will surely increase the chances of responsive and accountable government. And, given just how big the slice of the electoral pie is that the ANC still gets, it is up to the DA to ensure our political system becomes competitive by offering voters an irresistible alternative to the ANC.

This is why I am fascinated by the prospects of the DA. Very few political journalists and analysts seem to take a close interest in the DA. While it is understandable – and even desirable – that most of our energy should be spent watching the government of the day closely, it is also important to get under the skin of political parties not in government. And often the DA is done a disservice. Even when the DA gets good coverage from the media, the quality of analysis about DA leadership battles and internal party disagreements about the big national issues tends to be poor.

Yet it's critical for the health of our democracy that we closely examine the official opposition. The DA is particularly interesting because it makes many unnecessary political mistakes that prevent it from doing better in elections than it currently does.

Of course, many will hasten to pull out the stats that show that DA support has climbed in recent elections in terms of what percentage of the votes it captures, an upward trend of which no other party (including the ANC) can boast. That retort misses the point: any political outfit that is serious about electoral excellence – and businesses make for good analogical cases here – would measure itself against the potential that it has, rather than simply bragging that the numbers are showing a trajectory in the right direction.

The truth is – given the ANC's deep leadership and ethical crises, the poor state of the state, and stubbornly high levels of inequality, poverty and unemployment – the DA really should get 30% of the vote in the next national and provincial elections in 2014. But I don't think they will. Not because the ANC is politically invincible. Nor, as some DA leaders believe, because black African voters suffer from Stockholm syndrome (if not sheer stupidity). But because the DA story is a comedy of political errors.

This book tells the story of these unnecessary political errors: a failure to properly understand its own liberal identity; a morally and strategically clumsy attitude towards race; a not-so-secret affirmative action programme for black leaders that is going pear-shaped; poor engagement with the ruling party; tone-deaf communications; and general confusion about whether or how to realign opposition politics in South Africa.

Many of these errors can be corrected. But most DA leaders respond to criticism with a vitriol and defensiveness that they usually think, ironically, their ANC counterparts have a monopoly on. What is clear to me, however, is that there are deep disagreements within the party and an opportunity to bring about internal changes that can turn around the fortunes of the party at the polls. In a sense, there is a battle for the soul of the DA going on, just as there is constantly such a battle going on within the ANC. It is called, well, politics. And so the extent to which tactical and other mistakes are likely to be rectified depends on how these battles play out. Time will tell.

* * *

Interestingly, as I neared the completion of this book and failed to keep word of it to myself, many friends, analysts, non-DA politicians, writers, journalists and members of the public struck up countless conversations with me about the title of the book.

There has been a fascination with the title 'Could I vote DA?', as opposed to, say, '*Should* I vote DA?' The other fascination has been with whether or not the book directly answers the question the title poses, with many wanting to know, 'So? SO??? What are you telling me to do, Eusebius?'

This is really interesting. It was becoming obvious to me as I wrapped up this project in late 2013 that many voters are as confused about where to put their crosses in 2014 as I was in that local elections queue in 2011. Hence the questions about whether or not the book's title is answered directly, and bluntly, in the very first sentence. I got some sense of the desire for the guidance we all seek, and the need to cut through the morass of political bull that is, often, the mainstream political discourse in our country.

There is confusion and even disappointment when I respond, 'No, I don't tell you how to vote. In fact, I am not yet sure myself if I will vote for the ANC, the DA, EFF, Agang SA, IFP ... or for none of these!'

At this point there is usually a stunned expression, a look that says, 'But what is the point of an entire book about the DA, dude, if you yourself by the end of the project have no conclusive answers whether you will actually vote for them?'

Simple. The book is an honest, subjective, thinking-aloud exercise about the range of issues that make me doubt whether I should go ahead and vote for the DA – from irritations with their tone to fears that they hate Black Economic Empowerment (BEE) as I do not, disillusionment about their leadership choices, dislike around how they engage the ANC, an assessment of their ideological foundations, etc.

And, like many of you reading this introduction, I am not psychologically enslaved by the glorious history of the ANC. I am capable of not voting for the ANC. I am, yes, capable of voting for the DA. I am just not sure whether I should. And the book systematically, chapter by chapter, analyses the range of issues and questions that will determine, for me, whether or not

I should take a chance on them.

Why am I not sure, even after writing the book? Because a week is a long time in politics. I am being economical with the truth a bit, though. I have, actually, *provisionally* reached a decision myself about the DA and whether or not to vote for them. But it is provisional.

Between now and the election there is still a lot of fluidity. For example, as I was writing this introduction, the DA was going through a confused little period about what the hell it really wants to say about BEE, with mixed messages coming from Mmusi Maimane and Wilmot James.

So, it is not so much that I haven't really made up my mind. Rather, much of what I have written about remained evident in the DA on a day-to-day basis, even as the book was being finalised, edited and put to bed.

But one should keep an open mind, right? So, that's about as much of an explicit answer as a political analyst ought to give, I think, about a likely voting preference.

At any rate, I don't think it is appropriate for books to prescribe voting choices, as much as it is acceptable for political writers to own and justify their perspectives on the political landscape. Voting preferences are necessarily deeply personal and reflect the unique values and priorities of each voter. I hope the value of this book, if it is of any value to you, is twofold.

One is to make you passionate about politics, which is often written off by too many people as boring or a necessary evil. I find politics deeply fascinating and an integral part of modernity as much as art, literature, music and media, say, have become elements of the human condition, even if they are social inventions.

In many ways the DA approaches politics as an exercise in number-crunching. In fact, here's a prediction: just watch how some of them will respond to this book as if the practice of politics – party politics – is the equivalent of a maths Olympiad exercise.

It is not. It is about life. It is partly constitutive of life. And the tone, style and subjective narrative of the book, I hope, brings that out. If I fail, it will not be because that isn't how intimate politics really is; I will have failed only because I haven't yet learned to write well.

The second, I hope, is that the book will help fellow confused voters to think aloud about the issues that will determine whether or not they should – or could – take a chance on the DA.

As for the wording of the title, my publisher and I wrestled a bit with options. There is something instructive about the title choice, which is related to my analysis of the DA. Why 'Could I vote DA?' rather than 'Should I vote DA?' The answer is simple really, and it can be found in a dinner conversation that happened on a Sunday night.

I was having dinner with two friends, one a black South African who grew up very poor in the Eastern Cape and who still has very poor family in the rural areas. He now lives in Johannesburg, a degreed professional, but with a profound awareness of his family's seemingly permanent poverty back home. Call him Jabu.

Our other friend, a North American, is a middle-class, well-educated guy, who had gone to top schools in the States and works here in South Africa at one of the world's best strategy consulting firms. Call him Jason.

Jason asked about my book, and how it was coming along. Like many others he wondered about the choice of the title. Why not 'should' rather than 'could'? He took for granted that I obviously *could* vote for the DA. He was in for a surprise. It is not obvious that anyone could vote DA.

He and Jabu proceeded to have a fascinating debate that I observed for a little while before joining. Jabu made his position clear: 'I could never vote for the DA.' The question, 'Should I vote DA?' does not arise for Jabu.

Now, what was also interesting to me as I listened to Jabu was how much of his justification was based on lies about the DA, but that is beside the point. He expressed deep fears about how right-wing, poor-insensitive and deeply uncaring the DA is. Some of the detail was true, but lots of it was false.

But the objective truth is not relevant. For the DA, the bottom line is that here you have an educated voter who does not like the ANC's record in government but who does not say, 'I could but will probably not vote DA.' He expresses a much stronger view: 'I could not vote DA.'

I tried, later on, to convince Jabu that he must be misspeaking, that surely he wants to be saying something less strong, something like, 'I could vote for the DA if they did X, Y and Z differently ...' He sort of budged, but not really.

At any rate, it is clear that some voters, like myself, are comfortable with the prospect of voting for the DA, but just do not know yet whether they will, in fact, vote for the DA. And then there are voters, many of them black, who do not like the ANC's governance record but who are not yet comfortable even *imagining* voting for the DA.

This book engages both sets of voters. And the DA, if it is smart, will do the same, instead of easily accepting that voters like Jabu are beyond its reach. I don't think Jabu is beyond persuasion. I think Jabu is one or two conversations away from reframing his thinking about the DA.

But that assumes that the DA is capable of reframing its own politics. We will have to wait and see.

1

DARLING, PLEASE PASS MY LIBERALISM

What's so scary about Ubuntu, anyway?

Is the DA even bothered by what most
South Africans think?

Is the DA open to change?

This chapter and the next examine the ideological foundations of the DA. I love talking about political ideology. But I know that not everyone does. And I am under no illusion that the 2014 election is not about to be determined by debates about political ideology – not in any overt or fundamental way, in any event. This is why I took seriously two responses I received from readers to an early draft of this chapter.

One was from a friend who said, 'Jesus, the chapter on liberalism is a bit parochial!' I actually never really had a precise understanding of the word 'parochial' to be honest, but because he is one of my sharpest friends I had to understand the feedback. So I finally got round to getting a proper handle on it.

And, fair enough, although an unusual application of the term, when fully explained, it sounded reasonable. His point was that only a handful of possible voters and readers would care for a chapter that discusses the ideological foundations of the Democratic Alliance. It is one of those specialist debates that will turn some people off. It will not decide someone's voting choice.

Put that reaction aside for the moment.

There was a seemingly different response from my publisher, Louise Grantham, who often spars with me during my writing bouts. Being a little more subtle than my rude lawyer friend, she suggested that perhaps we rearrange the furniture a bit and start with an 'easier' topic, like BEE, to get you, the reader, hooked and angry before expecting you to wade through a morass of ideological stuff. After all, we want to get to the crux of the issues that real voters care about. And so bread-and-butter and policy issues surely needed prioritising, she suggested.

Now, I say that Louise's response is 'seemingly different' because I suspect that she, just like my lawyer friend, fears that this debate is not crucial to voters. So why on earth make it the first chapter of this book? Why include it at all?

I disagree profoundly with both of them. Ideology should matter to you as a voter. This book, as a glance at the Contents page shows, contains what I believe are relevant topics, like popular policy debates. But voters shouldn't be engaged only by what they actually care about; they should also be engaged by what they *should* care about, even if they do not, yet, care about everything that affects them.

So let me briefly make my case for why ideology matters, and why it must be the basis for the 'easier' or 'sexier' debates that come later. Of course you need not read the book in chronological order – the chapters are mostly self-contained, other than this one and the next, which hang together as a pair – but here's why you might, actually, want to delay jumping to later chapters.

Ideology, if I can put it most basically, refers to those deeply held principles that inform the more specific choices we make in the public realm. When we decide whether or not the state should spend a lot of money on welfare, and how it should spend that money, our choices reflect deeply held beliefs that we do not talk about explicitly.

All you will hear in public, of course, is a guy arguing the merits of his view on welfare, but he will seldom say, 'I grew up in this kind of house, in this kind of community, and was in-fluenced by these thinkers that my lecturer Eusebius convinced me have the right outlook on politics … blah blah blah.' Actually the views we express about BEE, about welfare, about state-owned enterprises, about whether or not the state should impose more or fewer taxes … all of this stuff is based on the ideological commitments we have.

Everyone has ideological commitments. It doesn't matter if you don't know the academic words that describe your outlook. And it doesn't matter that you are not aware of your outlook. The fact is that by virtue of your life experiences you have an ideological outlook, and it is reflected in your views about the political debates that follow this chapter.

Now, here's the cool thing. If you took the trouble of ignoring my lawyer friend and Louise Grantham, and read this chapter to the end, you would realise that if we spent a bit more time directly debating political ideology, we might make progress on the more familiar debates, and more quickly. That is why it is worth improving the quality of political discourse in South African when it comes, specifically, to political ideology.

Here's a practical example from the media. Journalists often deny that their stories reflect ideological leanings. But take, for example, political journalist Karima Brown, and *Business Day* editor Peter Bruce. It is very clear to even a first-year Politics student that Brown has a deep commitment to socialism, and that Bruce is what we would call a libertarian.

Don't worry about the labels for now. The point is just that one really cool way of thinking about the country's problems would be to get Brown and Bruce to debate socialism versus libertarianism. All of their disagreements about the mining sector, taxes, corporate South Africa's responsibilities, etc. ... all of these flow from their fundamentally different ideological positions.

And like individuals, political organisations have ideological underpinnings. So I think we need to ask, 'What *is* the political ideology on which the DA is founded?' Or, more accurately still, 'What is the ideology that is reflected in their policies today?' If I am a socialist like Brown, for example, then maybe I never want to vote for the DA if it turns out that the DA hates socialism and is based on an ideology that rejects socialism.

If I am a right-wing libertarian, however, who believes in a small state, it might be music to my ears if it turns out the

DA is that party. In other words, I then know that I've found a political home that is committed to a political programme that reflects my ideological outlook.

And that, for me, is why ideology matters, and why it must be the very subject we interrogate about the DA before we drill down to the more familiar debates. It is too easy, really, to sell you chapters about headlines in newspapers.

Let's engage with ideology first.

A fascinating public spat played out in early 2013 between the DA's Deputy Federal Chairperson, Mmusi Maimane, and former DA staffer, Gareth van Onselen. This quiet and seemingly innocuous exchange, which got surprisingly little attention (publicly *and* inside the DA itself), is in my view a great example of a battle for the DA's identity that is playing out in the party. Here is how it all started and what happened.

In February 2013, President Jacob Zuma caused a stir by urging businesses to donate to party coffers with the incentive that these businesses' fortunes would 'multiply'. It was an irresponsible statement, conveying the impression that the party, and possibly the state, would reward those businesses that give money to the ANC.

There isn't something obviously wrong with the ANC as a political party favouring businesses that support its political programmes. In South Africa, however, the distinction between party and state is not yet deeply entrenched, which is why we see patronage networks and corruption across the various tiers of government. In that context, Zuma's message could reasonably be construed as a promise that even state tenders might be used to reward corporates that are loyal to the ruling party. And if that was not the message that Zuma intended to convey, then he was yet again guilty of some incredible and unnecessary misspeaking. But it is hard to believe that such plain language was unintended.

Enter Lindiwe Mazibuko, the DA's parliamentary leader. She argued that the remarks by Zuma 'severely compromise the principle of good governance, which our constitutional democracy fundamentally depends on'.[1]

She then increased the rhetorical force: 'This is further evidence of how President Zuma fundamentally confuses the role of the state and party, and how the government continues to misuse public money, which should be spent on the poor. The R250 million being spent on the upgrade of President Zuma's Nkandla residence is the most glaring example to date.' Thereafter she asked Zuma to retract his statement.

Unsurprisingly, Zuma was not fazed. But it was left to that most colourful of spin doctors, Jackson Mthembu, to deal with Mazibuko. (I had tried to get presidential spokesperson Mac Maharaj to explain the president's statement on 567 Cape Talk and Talk Radio 702 where I was a talk-show host at the time, but he declined the offer, giving me the technical rebuff that he does not speak for Zuma-the-ANC-president but only for

---

1 http://www.politicsweb.co.za/politicsweb/view/politicsweb/en/page71654?oid=350312&sn=Detail

Zuma-the-president-of-South Africa. I, too, would get tired of playing translator on a weekly basis.)

Mthembu, meanwhile, decided to sing from his favourite songbook, *The Spin Doctor's Collection of Personal Attacks*. He accused Mazibuko of simply not knowing African customs! Obviously this was partly intended to diss her as a *black* person. It is part of a sustained attempt to ridicule Mazibuko for not drinking the struggle-flavoured Kool-Aid that the ANC needs the black African majority to sip on until Jesus comes.

This is also why she has been ridiculed by Higher Education Minister Blade Nzimande for supposedly not growing up in a township, and it is the reason she is regularly referred to as a coconut by many ANC politicians and supporters. Even Julius Malema, the former ANC Youth League leader, once described Mazibuko, with childish glee, as 'Madam Zille's tea girl'.

So Mthembu was simply continuing in this vein: choosing personal attack as an easy, populist alternative to responding critically to the content of criticism. Why deal with a substantive concern about the connection between politics and money when you can attack the person making the point?

What happened next, however, was as unpredictable as a good twist in a *Generations* storyline. A black knight in shining blue DA armour by the name of Mmusi Maimane thought he would come to the distressed damsel's rescue. Little did he know as he was galloping towards Mazibuko that the biggest challenge ahead was not going to be the ANC's Mthembu screaming 'Coconut!' but a former DA comrade, a man from his own ideological camp, about to scream at *him*, 'Fake liberal! FAKE LIBERAL!' Friends and enemies are hard to distinguish in the political arena …

So Maimane wrote an article that was published in the *Sunday Times*. His main claim was that the ANC does not have a monopoly on what it means to be African. True Africanness for Maimane requires a commitment to Ubuntu. He argued that 'Africanness is defined by one's commitment to the issues and lives of the African people. And nothing can better measure that Africanness than one's commitment to the spirit of Ubuntu.'[2] Perhaps the heart of Maimane's position is expressed in his pithy summary sentence, 'Being African means being part of a community. And no one can take away our Africanness.'

What was left unsaid but implied, furthermore, is that the ANC was *undermining* Ubuntu, and that Maimane, as a black member of a party seen to be the vanguard of liberalism by many, does not have to choose between liberalism and Africanness, nor between liberalism and Ubuntu. Black liberals can be authentically African, and they can champion Ubuntu.

Or so Maimane thought before the wrath of one Gareth van Onselen was unleashed!

In an article that dripped with venom, Van Onselen accused Maimane of committing the same sin as the ANC, that of telling others what it means to be truly African. If Jackson Mthembu is

---

2 'Being an African Extends Beyond Race', *Sunday Times* (20 January 2013).

not allowed to tell Lindiwe Mazibuko how to define Africanness *for her*, then who the hell was Mmusi Maimane to tell her to embrace Ubuntu if she wants to be *truly* African?!

That, in a nutshell, was Van Onselen's gripe. For good measure he also said that Ubuntu does not exist, and even if it did, it would be an alien value from which true liberals should defend themselves and their party. He implies in the end that Ubuntu is obtuse, and that the DA's liberal identity is at stake in this debate with Maimane.

Of course, Van Onselen's article was written in gentler language than I have used. This is important: it is emotionally safe to use technical terminology that gives the impression of dispassionate engagement. But politics is deeply personal. In reality, Van Onselen, like many established white liberals, is actually a tragicomic mix of *gatvol* and fearful when it comes to changes in the DA. His gripe with Maimane is important because it represents a rare public airing of private sentiment shared by many DA folks wondering where 'their' beloved party is headed with upstarts like Maimane being 'parachuted in'.

So do not be fooled by the traditional liberal's use of dispassionate language; there is serious battle being done here, and many glasses of wine being gulped down as these responses are typed out in response to talk about values like Ubuntu being married to liberalism.

The very identity of their party – *their* party – is at stake …

Van Onselen is a bit like an irate white parent at a Model C school in the early 1990s 'concerned' about the influx of children from 'different backgrounds', not because they are unwelcome – of course they are welcome, only Afrikaans white people on an *ossewa* are bigots, right? – but because 'the values' of the school might change. We can't have *that*, surely? Now – heaven forbid! – the school is in danger of having a black head prefect who thinks community is more important than the individual!

That kind of institutional anxiety experienced by some white parents at Model C schools in the early 1990s is similar to the anxieties that some long-standing members of the DA are now experiencing. This is not surprising. Change can be distressing. That is why change management is an industry worth billions the world over. Change within a political party is no less challenging than change within a complex business enterprise. Inside the DA, change is causing consternation among those who feel they own the institutional memory and political identity of the party. And that is why Van Onselen's schoolboy enthusiasm for thesis-long blog entries bemoaning change in the DA is significant, if laborious.

It is symptomatic of a perceived loss of identity, loss of power, loss of a political home.

And so, when Maimane tried to take on the ANC by publicly insisting that Mthembu was wrong, that black South Africans can be committed to Ubuntu and a deep sense of community, and still be members of the DA, Van Onselen lost his appetite. Why? Because Van Onselen did not hear a smart response from DA leader Mmusi Maimane who knows that the majority of this country is not liberal. Instead, Van Onselen heard in

Maimane's remarks a threat to a bygone era of a DA that did not have voters who cherished Ubuntu.

This raises two questions: is Van Onselen right to be dissing Ubuntu so badly? And, much more importantly – because, let's face it, you and I will not decide who to vote for based on what Van Onselen thinks – can the DA afford to ignore the values of the majority of this country if they want people to vote for them who previously have not done so? Let's consider each of these questions in turn.

IS VAN ONSELEN RIGHT TO DISS UBUNTU?

Van Onselen is correct in two regards.

First, Maimane was indeed guilty of essentialising African identity. I put it to Maimane in a radio interview shortly after his defence of Ubuntu that, surely, if I reject Ubuntu I should still be able to count as a member of the group 'African'. He fumbled.

He quickly denied not allowing diversity between black people. He denied imposing criteria for what it means to be an African.

And yet when I reminded him that in saying so he was re-tracting a key claim from his *Sunday Times* article, the claim that commitment to Ubuntu is the ultimate expression of Africanness, the closet debater in him pretended not to be contradicting himself. (I quoted him to help with the amnesia, 'Nothing can better measure … Africanness than one's commitment to the spirit of Ubuntu' – but most politicians are happy to reinvent the meaning of plain language when the alternative is to concede a contradiction.)

Maimane wanted to have his Ubuntu cake and eat it: keep the popular view that Ubuntu is an awesome African value we all should commit to as Africans, and at the same time be the familiar liberal who values individuals' freedom to self-define.

But if I have that kind of total freedom, then why tell me that I am not free to *reject* Ubuntu as part of my African identity? Van Onselen is right here: when Maimane prescribes Ubuntu as a value by which to live your life, he is behaving rather similarly to an ANC politician who thinks that real black people do not walk their dogs, speak with certain accents, or grow up in suburbs.

Ultimately, Maimane mimicked Mthembu while thinking he was criticising Mthembu.

Secondly, Van Onselen is also right to take a dig at Ubuntu as a concept, although his criticism is underdeveloped. Van Onselen simply asserts, for example, that 'ideologically and so far is (sic) liberalism is concerned, there is no such thing as Ubuntu'. This is intellectual laziness of the worst order for someone who often takes childish delight in spotting even a missing comma from the texts of people he engages.

First, you cannot simply claim that it follows from the definition of one ethical theory that another does not exist. That is fallacious. To do that is simply to *assert* that Ubuntu is not coherent without constructing an argument to that end. Such is the disdain that some have for concepts that are rooted in indigenous knowledge systems. You can only construct a full counter-argument against a concept if you take that concept remotely seriously. The subtext here is, 'Ubuntu, dude? Be serious man! I'd rather watch paint dry than spend a whole day thinking about that rubbish!'

Van Onselen's attitude highlights the need to find a way of making sure that the arrogance of a cultural minority does not turn off those whose values are not in the founding documents of the DA.

Second, Van Onselen suggests that because there is scarce practical evidence of Ubuntu, it does not exist. This is palpable nonsense. It is like saying that because Christians sometimes do bad things, there is no such thing as Christianity …

Whether it is coherent or useful or adequate as a basis for building society are different matters. But to say Ubuntu does not exist is to either speak mumbo jumbo about the nature of theory, or to impose metaphysical expectations – rather bizarrely – on Ubuntu that you do not impose on liberalism.

It's not as though you say to your partner as you leave the house, 'Darling, please pass my liberalism?' The fact that Van Onselen questions the existence of Ubuntu speaks of the desperation of old liberals in the DA to ward off seemingly alien concepts from rural areas that are invading the beloved Democratic Party of old.

* * *

And yet I share Van Onselen's scepticism about Ubuntu. This book is not a philosophical exposition of Ubuntu, however, so I won't go into too much detail, suffice to say that for a couple of years now some of my philosophy colleagues have done an excellent job of taking Ubuntu seriously in the tradition of analytic philosophy. In particular, it's important to mention two of them: Thaddeus Metz, who is now the head of the Department of Philosophy at the University of Johannesburg; and Jason van Niekerk, who was in the process of having his doctoral thesis on Ubuntu examined at the time I was writing this book.

I do not think that there is anything unique in the substantive definitions – ethical theories, really – of Ubuntu that these philosophers develop, but what I have in common with Jason and Thadd is that I take conversations about Ubuntu extremely seriously. This is because my fellow South Africans take Ubuntu seriously, and to waspishly dismiss Ubuntu would be to arrogantly dismiss the world view of those who have a different take on the universe from mine.

It's for this reason that I take my colleagues' philosophical project seriously, and I think Jason is probably deserving of the title of doctor for the level of thought and analytic rigour with which he engaged the question of whether Ubuntu can, in the tough analytic tradition of Anglo-American philosophy, be stated as a coherent, self-standing, meaningful ethical theory.

The fact that I think they ultimately do not get there isn't crucial, philosophically. These kinds of critical claims about theories are made inside philosophy as a tradition all the time.

But here's the snag as far as Van Onselen and I are concerned. Don't you sometimes hate it – I'm sure you have had that feeling before – when someone else shares your opinion on something but you have a sneaking suspicion your bases for the opinion are very, very different? Or that the opinion will play very different roles in your respective lives? And you want to distance yourself from what they want to do with the opinion you both hold?

Think for example of a mom who might insist that her daughter not wear skimpy clothing out that might get men overly excited about her precious young daughter. Many deeply conservative men – and women – may agree, and egg mom on to forbid Joanne from wearing that skirt. But the motives could be very different. It is possible that mom really just wants to minimise the chances of her daughter being assaulted by sexist pigs at the Bree Street taxi rank. And although usually not one for arguing that men should control what women wear, on this occasion, a basic motherly impulse not to want to get a call from a hospital about her daughter might have triggered the insistence that Joanne change into 'safer clothing'.

But the neighbour who was affirming the mom's message might, for example, believe that it is utterly immoral for girls to show a bit of flesh, that women should never show parts of their body in public, and that women should not tempt men to assault them, say.

This is all hypothetical. But the point is that it is very possible for two people to express the same opinion, but they could hold such an opinion for very different reasons and motivations. That is what is important in the context of this chapter. What is the motive behind the seemingly nerdish critique of Ubuntu by some people in the DA?

Motives, and reasons for holding viewpoints, and who holds certain viewpoints, are awkward social realities that can be very illuminating, however difficult it can be to get a clear grasp on motive without being, well, a shrink.

But let's venture there …

When I read the words of Van Onselen in response to Maimane, and sense the desperation to save *his* DA from non-DA values, then I fear something else is going on. And of course I am no shrink, no Dr Phil. I concede that this is speculative territory. Which is why I toyed with self-censoring this part of my reaction to the exchange between Maimane and Van Onselen. But the reality is that politics is not an exercise in rational-choice theory. It is often the stuff of emotion, even for number-crunching pollsters once they get inside the voting booth. And so what's most useful is to expose how I reacted as a voter, as a citizen, not as political analyst. Because as a political party the DA needs to get a sense of how, in real time, voters feel and respond to it.

I saw in Van Onselen's excessive, thesis-long response to a simple, well-meant little article by Maimane, fear. It is the fear of a white liberal with a history in the DA who feels liberals will lose something they own if they do not fight for it. It is the familiar fear of a loss of power on the part of those who have always had power. It is the arrogant, uncritical desire to continue to dictate the norms and identities of institutions that have never seen outsiders enter them. It is, frankly, a case of, 'How dare you, Mmusi! Aren't you grateful enough we even let you in in the first place and gave you some nice titles?! Wasn't that enough, mate?'

And that is why it grates me that my intellectual scepticism about Ubuntu coincides with what some liberals in the DA might say. Because I think the brutal truth here is that many of these liberals are motivated by a feeling of impotence in the face of new values competing with their old, established values.

And, going back to my earlier argument, it all makes me wonder, 'DOES IT EVEN BOTHER THE DA THAT I FEEL THIS WAY?'

So, where does this leave the voter? Or can the DA afford to ignore the values of the majority?

In order to vote for the DA, let alone even imagine the DA as a political home (which is a heavier commitment), I would have to find the identity of the DA attractive. This is why I am discussing political identity right up front. I don't think I am unique in this regard. Obviously the DA would love us to be in a future in which identity and memory played little or no role in voters' political choices at the ballot box, but we do not live in that kind of world. The DA has accepted that it has to work with the psychologies of voters who actually exist. It cannot work with the psychologies of future voters.

This is why the DA decided in April 2013 to start the 'Know Your DA' campaign. It is aimed at challenging the ANC's hold on struggle history by punting narratives of DA heroes who also contributed to the liberation of the country from apartheid. That strategy is an acknowledgement that identity and memory matter to voters.

But identity is not just about history. Identity is about an enduring set of moral values and principles that guide my daily life choices. It is about the values that lie at the heart of my character. And I want a political party to be at least broadly compatible with my fundamental values and general political outlook.

Politics in South Africa is not only about bread and butter. Perhaps it should be. But it is not. It is heady, emotional stuff; it is deeply personal. Political parties must capture voters' imaginations, and not just throw data at them. That is why it will never be sufficient for the DA to show voters audited data about underperforming ANC public servants. The DA itself, as a political machine, must also, in addition, be a psychologically appealing entity. That is a horrible burden for a party that desperately wishes it only need trot out PowerPoint slides when engaging communities. But such is the reality of politics in a country with our history: politics is life.

Here is the main political identity point: the DA has to decide. Will it make the undecided voter, the new voter, the prevaricating voter, part of the dialogue about the political identity of the DA? Or, will it let a few members of the old liberal gang continue to dictate the identity of the party?

And let's be clear here, as political analyst Aubrey Matshiqi once put it: one can be part of the numerical majority but still be part of the cultural minority. The DA thinks that images of more black Africans at rallies – and even in some of the leadership structures – implies transformation. It does not. Demographic shifts are necessary, but that's not enough. The institutional identity has to change too, and become more inclusive.

This is also why, by the way, it's no use screaming at this page if you're a DA fan and saying, 'But I know soooo many people in Alex, Eusebius, who are black like my gardener and yet are members of the DA!' Just like many black kids do not go back to Model C school reunions despite black kids now being the numerical majority in these schools, so having black Africans in large numbers isn't sufficient to signal institutional and organi-sational change. (Black kids will regard themselves as 'Old Boys' when they feel a sense of ownership of these schools; cosmetic, numerical changes aren't enough, in case you're wondering.)

Change has to be more fundamental, and this is what I'll wrestle with in the next chapters.

Yet, as the Van Onselen–Maimane spat shows, the voter is nowhere to be found as the DA searches for a party identity fit for the year 2014 and a 30% vote at the next general election. Is the DA still simply a classic liberal party of old? If so, what is the attraction for millions of illiberal, socially conservative voters to climb aboard? If the DA is economically liberal, where is the room for a voter deeply committed to an interventionist state to join up?

From basic philosophical foundations to specific policies based on those foundations, the debate about the identity of the DA is not a very open, public or inviting debate. The DA is not so much courting potential voters as much as they are telling potential voters what they are already firmly about. It is not clear how much fluidity there is within the DA to challenge or even change the party's political identity. For example, would the party be prepared to have potential new voters and members, ready to leave the ANC, come to the DA and debate whether the DA should remain a liberal party at all?

The debate should also include, as one friend pointed out to me, whether the DA is sufficiently liberal, by which I guess he means that there are different ideas about what liberalism is, and the party needs to have that discussion too. I, for example, consider myself an egalitarian liberal, and that is a strand of liberalism that allows me to be committed to the rights of individuals and minorities – in the context of appreciating freedom as foundational to liberalism – while also being committed to social outcomes like substantive equality and social justice. This is why I am irritated when the likes of South African Communist Party leader Blade Nzimande, who knows better as a well-educated politician, pretends that there are no strands of liberalism able to commit themselves to justice and substantive equality.

But here's the crucial point: when so many older people are territorial about the DA that they think it belongs to them just because us blacks never, historically, belonged to liberal parties in large numbers, then where on earth is the incentive for a Eusebius to feel comfortable – I repeat, to *feel comfortable* – going near the party structures?

The DA, it seems to me, may not be open to debating its established liberal foundations. A disillusioned ANC voter, or a new voter who doesn't have liberal instincts, may not yet be comfortable with joining the DA or voting for it.

Unless, of course, the DA developed a more inclusive political identity.

Is that possible? Can Ubuntu, or some form of communitarianism, live side by side with liberalism? I think so. And in the next chapter I show just how that is possible.

But don't get excited too quickly if you are a voter keen on joining a DA that respects your commitment to Ubuntu. I am not convinced the party gets the importance of a more inclusive political identity. So it may be liberalism-as-usual for years to come.

Maimane might not have had the liberal arts skill to ward off the linguistic attack he came under from Van Onselen. He responded incorrectly and was rightly lampooned.

But no South African needs to choose between valuing her freedom to choose what kinds of life forms she wants to experiment with and settle on, and a commitment to family, community or society.

What are the implications of all this for the DA? It's simple really. Speak an inclusive language when it comes to ideology and values, and mean it. And not just because that makes tactical and practical sense (you want the masses to vote for you even if three disgruntled diehards from Krugersdorp leave the party), but because it makes liberal sense to be more inclusive. It's rubbish, as I will show, to suggest that the party is selling its soul by accommodating values like Ubuntu or, if you want to disparage the U-word, by accommodating the, uhm, *language* of Ubuntu.

The moral, frankly, is simple. Liberalism requires you to accept values like Ubuntu. If you don't, it's either because you're a closeted illiberal or a liberal scared of losing power. Making Mmusi feel comfortable with his Ubuntu-talk is the liberal thing to do.

2

IF I'M INTO UBUNTU AND STUFF, CAN THE DA BE MY POLITICAL HOME?

What does liberalism mean anyway?

Can the DA accommodate illiberal liberals?

Why do some older DA members fear the growth of the party?

For one DA politician I met, his very career is up for grabs when non-liberals start swelling the ranks of the party in Gauteng. His sexuality, comfortably fitting in a liberal society, doesn't fit quite as easily in a more complex DA with lots of non-liberals. Equally, for someone like Gareth, if we cut through the intellectual bull, there really is a lot of personal fear that partly motivates the relentless resistance to keep the liberal fort, well, classically liberal.

The debate about liberalism is also personal for outsiders thinking of joining the DA. If, for example, you struggle a little to get 'into' the very issues that liberal debates are about, then you are probably one of the voters for whom, as my lawyer friend predicted, some of the stuff in the previous and this chapter will come across as parochial. But this too is instructive. Because it means that the DA will be unattractive to you too, on a personal level, in part because you *do not speak the language of liberals*. So even a lack of familiarity with these debates will give you a sense of how difficult it can be as a disgruntled ANC voter, say, looking for a comfortable new space. It is, to return to an earlier analogy, like us kids literally and figuratively learning the language of Model C kids in the early 1990s.

Which is why the central issue in this chapter is whether or not the DA can be a comfortable space for outsiders to access. Let's explore this question by starting with the story of the politician I referred to earlier.

Last year I wanted to do a profile interview on radio of an interesting DA MP, Ian Ollis. Purely by coincidence, the interview was scheduled for the week before the Gauteng elective conference of 2012. Ian was running for the top leadership post. I told him that I was not interested in connecting the interview specifically to the leadership contest. It was a profile of him as a politician, his life, his career and, specifically, what it has been like for him as a gay man inside the body politic in South Africa. I knew that he was gay, perhaps even comfortably gay in our interactions, but it was not something that featured centrally in his public life. And of course it does not need to. Why should it define him? But I was going to ask him, among other questions about his life, what it was like being a career politician as a gay man in a country that is deeply homophobic.

He was very keen. But he hadn't always been keen. He knew though that it would be hard to justify not ever wanting to talk about sexual identity. And, I guess, Ian could take comfort in the fact that he was not about to get bigoted treatment on the matter from his interviewer. I am openly gay, and have on-the-record convictions about homosexuality and public life that are progressive (I hope), so the engagement on the issue would not leave him exposed. At any rate, the slot on my radio show where the interview was to fit in was known for trying to get to know people intimately, as rounded human beings. Their friends and family are set up to call in, I play favourite and influential music from key moments in their lives, read and discuss their literary influences, etc. It is not a grilling. It is, in the most classic sense of the term, profiling. So Ian tentatively agreed, before hitting the pause button on his enthusiasm a day or two later, suddenly saying he would first have to speak to his campaign manager, senior DA MP James Lorimer.

I was excited until then. I don't think enough gay people in positions of power live openly. And a number of gay politicians, both in the DA and the ANC, pretend to be straight, so Ian would not only role-model authenticity, he would actually be doing his party a huge political favour by being the first politician to do so. It would be a scoop for me as radio host, a win for the gay community, good radio (complete with shades of discomfort) for my generous listeners and, for what it was worth, his party needed not be nervous either, surely? Or, so I thought. WRONG!

James advised Ian *not* to go ahead with the radio interview. I was shocked and intrigued. The party leaders reckoned that there were so many homophobes inside the DA that it would ruin Ian's chances of becoming the DA's provincial leader if voting delegates found out on radio the week before the provincial elective conference that Ian was gay. It would be just the extra help that John Moody needed to beat Ian.

If the radio host in me was disappointed, the political analyst in me was jumping up and down like a little kid with behavioural problems. This was bloody tantalisingly brilliant gossip about what senior leaders of the DA think of their members. DA leaders fear that there is a critical mass of homophobes inside the DA? Wow. I thought the ANC had a monopoly on bigotry. At the very least I would have thought that the DA thought that the ANC had a monopoly on bigotry. (As it happened, of course, Ian lost the race anyway.)

I am not sure whether Ian and James are right that the DA's voting delegates' homophobia would shape their voting choices. That is pure speculation on their part. And I guess they wanted to play it safe on the eve of the election. But what I do agree with entirely is their hunch that many DA supporters are no different from ANC supporters in their attitude towards homosexuality.

We often spend a lot of time in our country – other than during moments of international sporting euphoria – wondering about the things that divide us: race, class, income, language, geography, and political affiliation. We spend way too little time, however, on an equally curious question. What do millions of us have in common?

Many South Africans are united in illiberal attitudes towards moral questions like whether or not homosexuality is acceptable. A DA supporter in the township might squabble with an ANC supporter about whether or not Helen Zille is fabulous when they wear their respective party T-shirts. But put them in their regular clothes, forbid talk of party politics, and solicit only their viewpoints about gay sex or lesbian relationships, and you will see common values surfacing between them.

But there is more: this is a not an observation only about poor black South Africans. The casual homophobia of witless middle-class white men like David Bullard and Jeremy Gordin in their columns on politicsweb.co.za about the 'gay mafia' fascinates me too. That is also instructive. David, for example, thinks it is fun to defend the homophobic actions of businesses that discriminate against gay couples with whom they do not want to transact just because they are gay. It does not matter that the law disallows such discrimination. The law ruling out irrational discrimination is an abomination, apparently (go figure). By contrast, the arbitrary discrimination by the business owner should, for David, be allowed.

I wonder if David would feel the same about businesses wanting to discriminate only against former columnists accused of racism. Such is the uncritical nature of illiberal attitudes towards minorities and individuals, even among supposedly educated natives.

Similarly, Jeremy Gordin, in torturously unfunny copy, relentlessly goes after constitutional law expert Pierre de Vos, who simply explains the content of the law and its application (and happens to be gay). These personal attacks from Gordin, masquerading as wit, remind me of the casual prejudice 'weaker' boys might encounter at the hands of matrics in a boarding school.

Lesbians in our townships get raped and killed by ruthless homophobes. Gordin's victims do not die. He uses words. But verbal violence from English-speaking, middle-class white South Africans against gays unites these writers in their illiberalism with the township thug. The outcomes differ. The underlying moral values do not: homophobia, illiberalism.

Here is the point: even seemingly educated, wealthy, well-travelled, seemingly cosmopolitan, white, well-read, suburban-dwelling South Africans have a disdain for the rights of gay people to enjoy their freedom to live as equal citizens next to their straight counterparts in South Africa.

Jeremy Gordin, David Bullard, the ordinary DA supporter, the ordinary ANC supporter, and the maid and gardener whom Gordin and Bullard imagine to be fundamentally different in kind to themselves, all share a profound commonality: illiberalism.

And homosexuality is just one example – we could as well discuss the spanking of kids, abortion, death penalty, who the head of the household is or should be (mom or dad), whether our teen daughters should be allowed to wear miniskirts, the importance of religion, whether respecting elders matters, the role of traditions, etc. There will not be consensus on all of these themes but there will be a predictable pattern here: liberals are a minority.

Most South Africans care about family, church, community, society, tradition, and individuals *not* obsessing about their individualism at all costs. And, as the DA grows, its ranks too are being swelled by South Africans who are not liberal.

James Lorimer and Ian Ollis know that. The question this raises for the DA now, however, is this: can the DA accommodate South Africans who are not liberal? I think so. I also think the party can do so *in the name of liberalism rather than in the name of winning votes.*

The DA *can* have an inclusive political identity, one that accommodates South Africans with diverse moral and political instincts. Unlike many critics of Ubuntu or conservatism fear, an inclusive identity does not mean a broad church devoid of any non-negotiable principles and values. It is not a case of 'anything goes'. Liberalism can remain while the moral outlook of a diverse group of South Africans can be accommodated. Old liberals need not run for the hills when they hear the word 'Ubuntu'.

One crucial premise throughout this chapter is actually a liberal one: liberalism, properly understood, requires a more serious effort than is currently being made by the DA to accommodate the moral and political outlook of people fundamentally different from the party's founders.

In other words, much of the fear of people like Gareth van Onselen turns out upon closer inspection to be deeply illiberal! Let me get to these conclusions step by step, starting with a near definitional impossibility: what *is* liberalism, anyway?

LIBERALISM 101

Liberalism has unfortunately become something of a swear word. Many of my friends whom I regard as liberal would be mortally offended if I described them as such. Some people think only whites can be liberal, often imagining the term to apply to paternalistic whites who think they know what is good for everyone including, and especially, their black buddies. Others immediately think 'DA' when the word 'liberal' is mentioned, which is part of their motivation for rejecting the label, fearing that it boxes you politically.

All of this is unfounded. These stereotypes are simply a consequence of the bastardising of the word. The only thing to be said in mitigation of the word's horrendous use and abuse in political debate is that most political terms suffer the same fate.

That is what happens when everyone uses a word with gay abandon – it loses meaning, it changes meaning and takes on different meaning in different political contexts. Some liberals are so fed up with this verbal abuse that they recommend we stop using the term altogether. The recommendation is based on the fear that no two people will have the same meaning and sense in mind when they talk about 'liberalism', so why have a sloppy conversation? Why not consign the word to the dustbin of history?

I think that is a melodramatic response to the problem. For one thing, many words in our political lexicon would have to be ditched if multiple and contested meanings drove us crazy so readily. For another, why not simply say what you and others mean at the outset of a discussion? Then you can make sure your agreements and disagreements are genuine, and not just a semantic disagreement. There is nothing wrong with simply stipulating, for purposes of discussion and debate, what you take liberalism to mean.

After all, it is not the word that ultimately matters. It is the *thought* that you wish to convey that matters, so if you're clear about your meaning upfront, then there shouldn't be confusion in a discussion about liberalism. And that is really the best way to proceed here.

I will sketch my own understanding of liberalism. It is not the only definition of liberalism. Some might even argue, for reasons I am not interested in pursuing here, that it is not even the best account of liberalism. That really does not matter deeply. It just is the kind of political vision of what I, Eusebius McKaiser, mean by liberalism that I want to express. So I make no pretentions about offering an exhaustive or critical account of everything political theorists and philosophers have had to say about liberalism. This is not the place for that kind of exposition.

I am, however, confident that the kind of political arrangement that I will sketch – the statement of what the moral limits on state power should be, and an account of the relationship between individuals and the state, and the importance of individualism – will intuitively be recognised by theorists as a typically *liberal* arrangement.

The philosopher I reference most often when I explain why I call myself a liberal is John Stuart Mill. In particular, his classic essay, *On Liberty*, provides a useful blueprint for a liberal society. It sets out what kinds of powers are morally acceptable for a state to have in order for that state to be properly regarded as liberal. That essay, more than any other publication, captures what I mean by liberalism. It is old, much has been written about it and many contemporary philosophers have developed the foundational insights and quibbled about them, but I remain convinced that as a basic exposition of a liberal society, it is more or less spot on. So, what is my Mill-inspired idea of liberalism?

The most basic ingredient of a liberal society, in my view, is a society in which individuals are deeply respected as capable of deciding for themselves what values they want to adopt as the basis upon which to live. In practice, this might mean, for example, that I am an agnostic, selfish bastard who reads a lot of literature, places as much if not greater value on friendships than on biological family relations, and little or no value on church, religion, the state, community or wider society, beyond paying taxes, complying with the law, and following what I regard as genuine moral requirements like empathising with those worse off than me.

But really no one – not the state, not my dad, not my mentors, not my favourite school teacher, not my favourite writer – tells me, Eusebius McKaiser, what kind of life to live. I am free, in a liberal society, to make up my own mind.

It is not, though, a case of freedom for its own sake. There is good moral reason why my freedom is respected in a liberal society. Because, as an individual, I am best placed to know what I want and what I value.

Most people reading this book have not met me, have not lived my life, have not gone through the ups and downs that I have gone through, or experimented with Catholicism, flirted with homosexuality, assessed Ayn Rand's egoism philosophy, etc. In other words, you are not me, and you have not lived my life. Only I am in a position to assess what really matters for me, and to me.

So why the heck should you be prescribing values, or even principles, by which I should live my life? It does not make sense, does it? That is the rationale behind the liberal state's respect for the autonomy of the individual: a government, far removed from the details of the lives of Sipho, Kobus, Andiswa, Louise and Johannes, should not be so arrogant as to tell Sipho, Kobus, Andiswa, Louise and Johannes what to do and what not to do.

The role of the state in a liberal society is to make available as much space as possible for every individual to live an experimental life so that you might be able to discover, through a range of experiences, what it is that you value most deeply, so that you can make an informed decision about what you want to spend the larger part of your life engaging in.

What does this mean for government in practical terms, you might wonder? In a sense, the answer is simple: a liberal state should not moralise. It should rather provide resources that enable individuals to freely choose between various possible options. And the state should only ever restrict freedom, as Mill so elegantly argues, in order to make sure that one person does not harm another. That is the moral limit of state power.

State interference in our lives is only ever morally justified in order to protect other people's freedom.

This is why apartheid was immoral from a liberal viewpoint: the apartheid state restricted our freedom arbitrarily rather than only to prevent people from harming each other. When we were prevented from living where we wanted to, this was not done to prevent harm to others. It was done for no rational reason at all. It was done simply to suppress us.

In a nutshell, then, a liberal society celebrates the individual as a mature creature who should be allowed the space to fashion her own identity and projects as she goes through the tough but rewarding business of living an experimental life. Liberal states err on the side of allowing freedom, and the burden is always on the state to justify why freedoms should be restricted.

And when the state wants to restrict some people's freedoms, it must be able to prove that the restriction is necessary in order to prevent harm to others.[3]

In South Africa we have done quite well – depending on

---

3 In Mill, of course, there is a complex and detailed discussion about these concepts including the so-called Harm Principle. Scholars disagree about what counts as harm and, so, what counts as legitimate instances when states can encroach on the general freedoms of citizens. It is beyond the scope of this chapter to give a faithful academic exposition of these fascinating debates or to stake clear academic positions within them.

whether or not you are a disciple of Mill as I am – to have crafted a Constitution for a democratic South Africa that essentially aspires to build a new society that is, at its core, a liberal society. Constitutional law students would not disagree deeply that the Bill of Rights, for example, places fundamental emphasis on founding values like the intrinsic self-worth of every individual, self-worth that can never be violated, never be trumped by group rights. This is known as the right to dignity. While it is true that, as South Africa's constitutional jurisprudence has developed over the years, the Constitutional Court has tried to balance individual rights with societal interests, there is a general presumptive bias in favour of individuals and minorities against the brute untested preferences of a numerical majority of citizens. This is unsurprising: it is the philosophical influence of liberal individualism in the expressed and underlying values and clauses of our country's Constitution.

It surprises me that occasionally I meet politicians, commentators and scholars who resist a characterisation of the South African Constitution as liberal. I think they confuse the question: 'Is it a liberal document in essence?' with the very different question: 'Is it regrettable that the Constitution is essentially liberal?' The answer to the first question is surely uncontroversially 'yes' while the second is a question reasonable people can disagree about.

But here's the snag for the DA: despite the fact that the idea of a liberal society is compelling, based on Mill's nifty little argument for why individuals should be left alone, and why the state should not interfere in our lives without bloody good reason, all of which is embodied in our wonderful Constitution, our society is not liberal! There is a gap between Mill and South Africa. There is a gap between our Constitution and South Africa. There is a gap between the DA and South Africa. Put simply: we live in a country in which the liberalism of people like myself is alien to many fellow South Africans.

And so an argument for a liberal state, and in defence of our liberal Constitution, may be philosophically convincing but could still be politically disastrous for the DA. The DA needs to engage the country we live in, not the philosophical texts liberals revel in. And if the point of being a political party is to get into power first, and then do good things with the legal and political power once in, then you have to engage the actual moral values and outlook of the majority. Mmusi Maimane is probably also not the typical voter. Mmusi's emotional and linguistic dexterity with words, concepts and values like 'Ubuntu' position him closer to the voters who are not voting for the DA currently than the blogger writing about Mmusi's Ubuntu-speak. And if senior leaders in the DA do not recognise this fact, and ask themselves what the consequences are for electioneering, then they kiss a 30% election voting target goodbye.

But here is the good news, to rush to the end, before slowing down the story again: the DA does not have to ditch its commitment to liberalism in order to attract black voters. I actually think that many people have a profound – and irritating – misunderstanding of the meaning of liberalism. A deep commitment to liberalism requires, as Mill is at pains to explain in the middle sections of *On Liberty*, accepting difference, accepting a plurality of lifestyles, outlooks on life, and only a broad overlapping consensus in principles.

So in a strange way, the reason why Mmusi's Ubuntu-speak should be accommodated is not to attract more votes. It is not a pragmatic reason. Actually, Ubuntu-speak should be accommodated in the DA because liberalism, as a matter of political philosophy, demands that the party respects diversity. Van Onselen, in the end, is a fake liberal.

And if he is not a fake liberal, then he is surely misrepresenting his understanding of liberalism out of sheer fear that he will lose political and ultimately economic power if the gates are open for people to enter a place where only whites had previously ruled.

Nevertheless, let me explain why I think Van Onselen's conclusions about Maimane are right, even if they are motivated in his case, in my opinion, by an existential crisis about changes inside the DA.

First, there seem to be as many different definitions of Ubuntu as there are people who care to have a crack at telling us what it is. This is a sure sign that a concept is vague, and that anyone can project onto it whatever they had for breakfast. Obviously concepts can be contested: indeed, one of the best examples of such contestation is 'liberalism' itself.

But Ubuntu suffers unforgiving vagueness. The most

consistent sort of thing you hear about Ubuntu is that it refers to 'humanness' or 'respect' or perhaps 'caring about others and not just your individual self'.

But why is caring about others or being humane unique to Africa? I have met some pretty selfless people while living in England, many of them coming from all over the planet. Equally, we all know many egotistical, selfish individuals who were born here. And Robert Mugabe is not the only example. So there is nothing *unique* about humanness or consideration for others' interests being observed in sub-Saharan Africa.

Many defenders of Ubuntu think they have picked out a moral value that is genuinely new, rather than just a word for something that is universal. But if humanness and selflessness can be found everywhere in the world, then what is so unique about Ubuntu? It seems as if Ubuntu is just another word then for a familiar universal value that can be found in all languages and in all societies.

Of course, the friends of Ubuntu can always change their minds. Instead of insisting that Ubuntu is a unique ethical theory not found anywhere in the world, they can simply claim that, yeah, sure, it is not unique to Africa but it is *more prevalent here* than in societies like those in Western Europe where individualism is more rampant.

Will this do? Two problems then raise their anti-Ubuntu heads: for one thing, only some fans of Ubuntu would be happy with this change in position; the majority, I suspect, would insist that Ubuntu is not just empirically more prevalent in Africa but *really, really* does refer to a unique ethical theory. For another, it would be a huge concession for sceptics like myself if someone admitted that Ubuntu is not special but just more popular in Qunu than in Los Angeles.

That's about as interesting as saying romance happens every-where but is particularly *the* thing in Paris. It becomes cultural anthropology, and little else.

And yet even as an empirical or anthropological claim there are problems: has anyone ever really tested whether Africans are more selfless than Western Europeans? When I had this dis-cussion on radio, one of my listeners tried to give me evidence: 'Eusebius, in the township, if you run out of sugar, you can get it from your neighbour! There in the suburbs you guys don't even know the names of your neighbours!' He obviously meant that the township in this story is a place where the spirit of Ubuntu is alive and well, and our suburbs are replicas of the individual-ism that epitomises life in Western Europe. And, in the context of the DA debate, the township values that Maimane was punt-ing cannot, for this listener, be married to the selfishness that Van Onselen was batting for.

But my listener romanticises township life. And he caricatures sub-urban life. He is no different to professors in Anthropology and Sociology who do the same but with more obscure linguistic tools. I grew up in a poor neighbourhood. While we often expe-rienced and exhibited a great sense of community – helping out a family that had a bereavement; massive wedding celebrations to which half the neighbourhood was invited even if it was madly expensive; school and church bazaars and community concerts; borrowing twenty rand from the family across the road for lunch for the school kids, etc. – there was also ruthless behaviour: murder, rape, stabbings, fighting in the street, fighting in the home, and less harmful evils like gossip and jealousy.

Yet we insist on descriptions of our townships as places where poverty's amazing spin-off is a unique degree of social bonding.

I find this, well meaning as it is, insulting. It perpetuates the idea that black people in particular do not care for individualism. We outsource our identities to that mystical thing called a group. That is rubbish. There is as much individualism among township dwellers as there is among the predominantly white residents of pre-democratic Sandton.

But just as we romanticise group identity among blacks and downplay individualism, we also do the opposite with the identities of people in other parts of the world. When I think of some of the men and women I have met in the twenty-or-so countries I have travelled to, including England where I lived for a few years, it would be grossly unfair to imagine that their generosity of spirit was a statistical anomaly, and that perhaps I had simply not encountered the majority of selfish, individualist bastards that make up most of North America, Europe and Asia. I might not have knocked at a stranger's door in England to ask for sugar, but plenty of times did I experience empathy and the support of friends, mentors, and even colleagues. Empathy for others and taking others' concerns into account when you act do not only manifest at giant township weddings and funerals. They can also be present in the breaking of bread with friends in London, taking in a down-and-out friend in New York, or drinking wine with a friend in Paris, soothing them after an emotionally shattering break-up.

No community anywhere in the world has a monopoly on either selfishness or individualism.

Nice people are everywhere. Bastards are everywhere.

LIBERALISM VS UBUNTU: A TIRED, FALSE DICHOTOMY

The implication of all this is that despite my sympathy for Van Onselen's critique of Maimane's thoughts on Ubuntu, ultimately, the spat between them simply demonstrates how pitting concepts like 'liberal' and 'Ubuntu' against each other can simply mess with the quality of public debate.

Liberalism is done a disservice because it comes out of this fight mischaracterised as selfishness or 'rugged individualism', as if liberals lack empathetic capacities or the ability to form bonds with others or even to have group identities or be members of various groups within broader society.

This mischaracterisation costs the DA. It explains why the caller I discussed earlier rejected Maimane's attempts to invite him into the DA with the incentive that Ubuntu fans can be liberal too. That caller did not want his values, and his foundational value of Ubuntu specifically, tainted by what he saw as a commitment on the part of liberals to individualism. But in rejecting Maimane's invitation, the caller exposed a deeply misguided view of liberalism.

Ubuntu too, already in definitional trouble for the reasons I hinted at, comes out the worse for wear. Ubuntu is ridiculed as a philosophy that does not have room for individual personality, let alone deeper value differences. You would swear nervous liberals think that a world in which Ubuntu is the official philosophy is a world in which people think, feel and maybe even look the same after a while. Such is the caricature in general of philosophies that place a fair amount of value on social structures. But no one thought that German philosopher Hegel, for example, believed that individuals should not exist or that individuals shouldn't be valued much just because he was a communitarian.

So why the habit here in sub-Saharan Africa of assuming that if you endorse a grounding value like Ubuntu you are endorsing a world in which we all look and think the same eventually?

Here's the bottom line: Ubuntu is at worst an incoherent ethical theory and at best an underdeveloped ethical theory. But to the extent that we can make sense of Ubuntu as a local variation on familiar communitarian philosophies found elsewhere in the world too, we can reject the battle between Ubuntu and liberalism.

The two philosophies are not incompatible. Liberalism promotes the idea of individuals and communities choosing values and lifestyles so long as they do not harm others. And if individuals choose to be guided by Ubuntu then a liberal state can accommodate that individual, and a community that chooses Ubuntu as central to its identity. There is no tension here.

The implication for the DA is this: the DA can accommodate the moral outlook of millions of South Africans who see and negotiate the world differently from those who founded the party. And it can do so philosophically, and not just as a matter of pragmatism.

Maimane and Van Onselen might be bedfellows yet. But it will require the old white liberals to stop fearing a loss of power if new values enter the party's round-table discussion. And the old white liberals need to stop misunderstanding what liberalism means.

3

PLEASE STOP SHOUTING AT ME

Can logic alone appeal to voters?

Why does the DA insist on dismissing all non-supporters as irrational?

Should the DA change the tone of its communications?

The past few years have been a fascinating personal journey for me when it comes to communication. I became a competitive debater in high school, mainly because I could not speak English very well when I started at Graeme College Boys' High in 1992. In fact, I was so bad at English that I refused to do my first class oral in Standard 6 – yes, that's what we called it back then – and settled for zero rather than have white kids laugh at my bad grammar and my shocking coloured accent. But I was also a very competitive *laaitie*. So I joined the debate club, to get practice in speaking English.

To cut a long story short, years later I was a competitive debater, who had travelled the world, and had won a national universities' debate title with my good friend Nick Ferreira while at Rhodes University. Many more years later I would win the World Master Debate title with Alex Just, a friend from Scotland I had met at Oxford University.

But here's the thing about debaters. Most competitive debaters are arrogant like DA politicians (though most DA politicians aren't as skilled in debate as competitive debaters of course), and most competitive debaters are as cocky as former DA researchers who think that constructing a logical knock-down argument on your blog, or in your *Business Day* column against Mmusi Maimane, makes you THE MAN. We delight, when we wear the competitive debater hat, in seeing an opponent verbally crushed.

Competitive debate is a little bit like rugby or boxing, but without the overt physicality. But don't get me wrong, it is profoundly intellectually and socially useful. In a future project I want to write about the nature of debate, and the need to get South Africans to debate more effectively. Hell, our bloody poor public discourse – especially in Parliament – could benefit from a simple, practical guide to effective debating. I would like to see every school in this country have a debate society, with a well-constructed debate curriculum.

But here is where I am going with this. There is a deep emotional disconnect between formal logic and the real world. There are shortcomings in the communication arsenal of someone who *only* uses the tools of formal logic to engage the universe. It doesn't connect with the headspace, and with the hearts of real people. It is cold. It can be degrading. It can, frankly, also lack *impact*. Logic, even perfect deductive logic, can be unpersuasive. Because human beings are not machines, but psychological creatures. So you have to appeal to them with more than just logic, and sometimes even with less than logic. If, that is, your aim is to change the world.

Let me give one personal example, before bringing us back more pointedly to the DA. I used to delight in being able to basically walk up to a whiteboard and construct the argument for homophobia:

Premise 1: Homosexuality is unnatural.

Premise 2: That which is unnatural is immoral.

Conclusion: Therefore homosexuality is immoral.

I would then proceed to dismantle this deductive argument as unsound – forget the meaning of these logical terms (that ability to dazzle with the use of the terms is itself part of the rugby game of verbal assault) – by showing why each of the premises is false, and why the argument for homophobia is not compelling.

I am sure many people who have issues with homosexuality would rather shut up in an audience than dare to engage me as I wield the weapons of logic.

But here's what I came to realise: I wasn't necessarily persuading homophobes to change their attitudes, to change their behaviour, for the simple reason that there is a gap between perfect logic and persuasion. It is called human psychology.

To get through to people you have to engage them as human beings. And so a major breakthrough for me, communicatively, and it remains ongoing, has been learning to speak from the heart – speaking about my life, how homophobia impacts me, my love for another man, and how it feels natural for me to desire same-sex intimacy. The power of this authentic testifying has done a helluva lot more to change the homophobic behaviour of some of my conservative friends than a textbook argument against homophobia.

I have basically had to realise the limits of formal, competitive debate, and I have had to learn a greater range of public speaking skills, and other communication devices. I have discovered the fun and beauty of the art of persuading and influencing people. It is a wonderful challenge for a cocky debater who thought being able to show off logic skills was all it took to get to the top of the world. Uhhm … NO!

* * *

Enter the DA. In a sense, the DA is a political party that basically behaves likes a high-school pupil who has recently become addicted to debating. They are not terribly good at it yet, but better than the lazy kids and plain untalented kids who are not in the debate club, and so with newfound cockiness they show off their debate skill.

You see it in the muscularity of an angry James Selfe rant, or even worse, an angrier Dianne Kohler-Barnard, who can be an assault on the eardrums. When I listen to these, and many other, DA leaders I get deeply embarrassed about my past as a competitive debater, both as a speaker, as well as a coach and a judge. Because both in the tone, and in the restricted techniques of the DA politicians within the debate arena of our public discourse, I see in a fresh way the horror of someone addicted to the diet of adversarial, competitive, debate-like communication.

And that is what I want to explore in this chapter. How the tone-deaf communication strategy of the DA costs the party. It alienates the party from voters who do not speak English well, for starters. It alienates the party from South Africans who do not worship the Westminster culture of politics the way I do. And, frankly, it gives unnecessary ammo to someone who wants to hold onto the belief that this party consists of a bunch of mostly white ageing leaders (and now some black ones too) who are shouting at the rest of us.

Let's take a closer look.

MAZIBUKO'S MISSED OPPORTUNITY

Early in 2012 I attended an event for young professionals hosted by the DA at the Rosebank Hotel in Johannesburg. Parliamentary leader Lindiwe Mazibuko was a big drawcard for many who had rushed from their jobs to be there in time. The atmosphere was great, and reminded me of the buzz many people experienced at the Congress of the People's events soon after its founding. There was a sense of optimism that Mazibuko, of the same age as many in the room, could convince those present that the DA was the perfect alternative to the ANC.

Sadly, Mazibuko did not have a sense of the burden resting on her shoulders. And during the question-and-answer session, an unfortunate incident was to play out. Two young women sat close to me. They were black, and could not have been older than about twenty one. One of them put up her hand and said she was studying at the University of Cape Town (UCT). She was about to graduate and feared that, as a black person, she might have some hurdles to jump in the corporate sector and so was a little scared of her prospects of entering the job market successfully. She was wondering what advice the DA had for a prospective black graduate with such fears, and would be grateful for some words of wisdom from Ms Mazibuko.

I cringed a little at the question because it felt a bit like a career guidance question. But I was cringing as someone who is *not* a politician. I was cringing as an anonymous member of the public. Lindiwe, of course, was on public display as an elected official of the DA, there to build her party's brand among young professionals. In particular, she had to try to increase the number of new voters for her party, especially among the young people and black people present that evening – by schmoozing. That's the business of being a politician, right? And, if anything, the question might have been a little high school-ish in its demand for words of wisdom. But it was actually a gift for an eloquent black woman; a chance to inspire a younger version of yourself. Easy as parliamentary pie. Surely?

Lindiwe responded rapidly, and with a fiery tone that astonished me, along the lines of: 'I'm surprised that anyone who is at UCT would have confidence problems. If you can get into UCT, then you should not have confidence issues. It is not my job to come to UCT and give pep talks.'

I was gobsmacked. As were the young ladies. I had never

seen enthusiasm drain from a face so quickly. And as soon as the question-and-answer session was over, they dashed for the exit, ignoring the free cocktails on offer. Lindiwe had surely lost the opportunity of turning the two young black women into DA disciples with her curt, thoughtless and heartless response to a perfectly sincere, if a little clumsy, request for job market advice.

Worse, many of us who were bystanders were irritated on behalf of the young woman. In that moment of responding to her, Lindiwe was addressing many black professionals who were not interested in the ANC Youth League – why else come to a DA event? They were, perhaps, not yet sure whether to 'take a chance' on the DA. Not every single person in the room was already a DA convert. But certainly almost everyone was prepared *to hear the DA out* – and therefore Lindiwe had to be savvy enough to know that everything she said, and how she said it, could determine whether or not she could convert possible DA supporters into actual DA supporters.

But, as was confirmed when I spoke to a number of people later, her response to the UCT student undid a lot of the good work of her main speech delivered earlier in the evening. The lesson, from a public engagement viewpoint, is clear: take particular care as a politician what it is you say and how you say it when you are not following the script of a prepared speech. Your true political character comes through most clearly during a question-and-answer session, and clearly that is exactly what happened – badly so – for Lindiwe that evening.

There is a more fundamental point to this story. As I wonder whether I could vote for the DA I wonder whether I could vote for a party that does not know how to communicate with me properly. When I have flashbacks of Lindiwe's response to that student, I think to myself, 'Typical DA! Arrogant! Shouty! Makes the voter's problem the voter's problem and not a DA or OUR COLLECTIVE problem!' Put simply, the DA is tone deaf. They haven't a clue just how incredibly know-it-all they come across as.

First, Lindiwe showed no empathy in that response. Rapid-fire sentences, loudly delivered, to someone who was having an existential crisis about their future in front of a huge crowd, does not show empathy for their plight. It shows a lack of humanity. It shows insufficient emotional intelligence.

Second, Lindiwe showed no understanding of strategic political communication in that response. If she had ever thought about the DA's communication weaknesses over the past few years, she would inevitably have come to the conclusion that, going back to the Tony Leon years, the DA has endured a public image of a party that is aggressive in its communication.

And so party leaders must now mix up the tone with which they communicate. Smile. Lower your voice. Sometimes show a bit of emotion. Nod your head in understanding of the young woman's troubles. If needs be, yes, even fake it a little bit, dammit. You are not in the business of authenticity as a politician. Politicians might claim, as a cheap electioneering ploy, to be sincere, but being a career politician is just another job. And one of the outcomes that you need to achieve is to persuade millions of voters that you feel them; that you empathise with them.

Lindiwe showed zero strategic communication sense that evening. She just showed how tone deaf she is. Like her party has been for years. And what this means, for me as a voter who is unsure about whether to vote for them, is that just as I come close to resolving that doing so might be a good decision for me and the country, I simply get irritated at being patronised, being spoken down to, being assumed to be dumb, being shouted at. Such is the stuff that comes from the mouths of most of the DA leadership. And it is a key reason why it is hard to fall in love with the DA. Sadly for the DA, these things matter. Politics is not only, as much as they wish it were otherwise, a matter of making rational calculations about the hard skills of respective parties' politicians and evaluating their different policy proposals.

If I sufficiently dislike you as a person, as a politician, as a political brand, then I might overlook policy considerations. You may call that irrational. But calling it irrational will not help you get into power. Change the tone of your communications.

ZILLE'S TONE-DEAF TWARS

I outlined the Mazibuko example in detail because it typifies the tone deafness of the DA. But frankly I have enough examples to fill several chapters. Who can forget, for example, Helen Zille's cringe-inducing insult hurled at artist Simphiwe Dana, in a twar (twitter war) about whether or not Cape Town is racist, during which spat she told Simphiwe in a tweet, 'You're a highly respected black professional. Don't try to be a professional black. It demeans you.' For a couple of weeks Zille had to endure the heat from black people on Twitter and was relentless in trying to defend herself instead of just crawling into a hole in acknowledgement of what was clearly an insult. To accuse a self-made success story and as brilliant an artist as Simphiwe of trying to behave like a 'professional black' was not just an insult for Simphiwe, but one many blacks would have felt too. The hundreds of angry Twitter responses corroborate this. That just is the reality of a country in which many of us young black professionals live – we constantly have to prove that we are successful not because we are black but because we are competent.

So by even hinting at the fact that Dana might trade on her blackness, using her blackness for economic or other gains, Zille had decimated a nerve in many a black Tweep. The reason, by the way, is that the term 'professional black' had appeared in a powerful column some time back in *Business Day* penned by writer and commentator Jacob Dlamini. In it, Jacob – rightly so in that context – took aim at those people who are black who leech off the state (and the private sector) by using their skin colour to act in cahoots with white business people needing a Black Economic Empowerment partner, say, or simply by crudely asserting it to be their turn to eat at the trough. In a state that is deeply corrupt, there really are professional blacks. And professional blacks make it hard for honest black professionals not to be second-guessed when they – black professionals – excel. And so when Zille thoughtlessly insulted Simphiwe – calling her an aspiring professional black – all hell inevitably broke loose.

But here is the moral: yet again a senior DA leader – this time the party leader – demonstrated an inability to communicate effectively with potential voters. Thousands of potential DA voters roam the streets of Twitter. Many are fed up with ANC corruption, arrogance and lack of service delivery. But they want the DA to prove to them that they are a worthy replacement for their loyalty. And so the DA, which has a stronger presence on Twitter than the ANC, has a chance to bowl over these disgruntled, possibly homeless voters.

The right tone, however, is crucial. What does Zille do? She enters into twar after twar, and calls someone a professional black – and not just anyone, for that matter, but a genuine black professional who is rightly a darling among black South Africans, the very constituency where Zille needs to make inroads.

It is not poor policy on the part of the DA that costs Zille potential voters on Twitter. It is tone-deaf communication, and an inability to say, 'Sorry, I insulted you, and I apologise unreservedly.' The DA just does not grasp the size of its communication errors. And the reason they do not grasp this is because they refuse to believe that coming after my vote is not just about policies and showing me the CVs of their politicians – it is about stealing my heart, speaking to me as if you take me seriously (and preferably *actually* taking me seriously), and not coming across like an arrogant know-it-all paternalist liberal. The DA needs savvy political communication. That is still sorely lacking.

THE ULTIMATE PROBLEM: ASSUMING I AM IRRATIONAL

I think the reason for the DA's tone deafness (and if not the reason for it, then certainly an implication of its tone deafness) is that it regards me, the hesitant voter or you the ANC supporter, as irrational. That is the only way I can make sense of why the DA is not patient enough to take me seriously, to sit down with me and converse with me, to laugh with me, to cry with me, and to wrestle with my outlook on life. It preaches at me instead. And so I have come to the conclusion that they behave in this strange, tone-deaf manner – even if it means I might not vote for them – because they think I am irrational. Let me explain.

I have had more debates with DA politicians than I care to remember about why it is that ANC voters keep voting for the ANC even though the same ANC voters protest about poor service delivery. They all come to the same view, even if they slightly vary the words they use: voters are irrational. Earlier in 2012, for example, DA MP Ian Ollis got frustrated in a Twitter discussion about e-tolls and in a fantastic burst of frustration – rare for him – tweeted to the effect that he is sick of telling people what democracy means. That it means if you vote for the DA you will not get e-tolls but that you would get them if you vote for the ANC. This is a typical DA attitude: accusing the voter who is not voting for the DA of not understanding democracy or, alternatively, characterising the ANC voter who votes for the ANC but who complains about the ANC government, as irrational.

This is just bizarre. Do we think of Labour Party members as irrational in England if they vote for Labour but protest the fact that Labour does certain things in government? Equally, someone might never ditch their membership of the Conservative Party but be deeply upset about Prime Minister Cameron's stance on gay marriage. But the DA deems it fit to casually regard millions of black South Africans as simply not understanding democracy or being irrational or voting against their own self-interest.

These convictions on the part of DA leaders underpin their tone deafness. They fuel their tone deafness. You can only become aware of your communication errors if you take the people you are 'communicating' with seriously. I am not convinced the DA takes non-DA supporters and ANC voters seriously – they are an irrational nuisance to be reluctantly persuaded.

Think, for example, of when you might shout at a child. You

do so because you do not think the child is sufficiently developed, cognitively, to be capable of dialogue. So why bother treating the child like an adult? In the same vein, a political party that shouts at me must be telling me that I am a child to be managed and not an adult to be engaged.

And so I have to wonder then whether the DA, when it speaks to me rapidly, loudly, and without empathy, and knowing all the answers to my woes, takes me seriously as a possible thought-partner? Or does the DA simply see me as a helpless subject in need of rescue? Because the tone and content of its communication suggest the latter. If Ian thinks I do not get democracy just because I do not, say, vote for the DA already, then Ian does not think I am particularly smart. And then I do have to wonder whether or not I can easily vote for a party that belittles my intelligence.

I might want a job, and a safe country where good opportunities flourish, but for better or worse, politics is personal for me, and for many South Africans. I want to be as comfortable with the political brand I vote for as I am comfortable with the car I might own or the suburb in which I buy a house. And the DA is sending me all the wrong signals.

SOME FINAL THOUGHTS: A QUIET EXCEPTION

One exception to the DA's tonal challenge is their national spokesperson Mmusi Maimane. Mmusi comes across as warm, affable, sincere, empathetic, self-critical, and open to dialogue and changing his mind. These are not communicative traits I associate with the vast majority of senior and public leaders in the DA. In some ways – as I discuss in a later chapter – Mmusi is an accidental politician. He is far more marketable than the rest, and they would do well to study his appearances on public platforms. Just watching his body language – mute the television, for example – is instructive. His face lights up, and he looks as relaxed as DA leaders like Dianne Kohler-Barnard or Helen Zille or Lindiwe Mazibuko do not. He breaks into an easy smile.

In fact, Mmusi succeeds in making it hard to be critical of him because he is so charming. Many of the criticisms of his leadership skill that I write about in a later chapter – which I have to write about to uphold my integrity as a writer – were, for a little while, difficult to pen because I thought of him in human terms rather than as 'politician'. I almost felt I was being unfair on him while drafting that chapter before checking myself, mentally, as an analyst.

It is easy to be seduced by a politician who is charming, and easy to go after a politician who thinks the voter should be oh-so-lucky to have their wisdom on offer. The DA, in Mmusi, has an example of the former, but is filled with way too many of the latter, more arrogant, kind of politician.

Unfortunately South African politics is a very muscular affair. And so Mmusi's communicative strengths will only get him so far in our public discourse if he does not develop a greater range of speaking styles. If Zille and Mazibuko need to learn to slow down and shout less when they speak, and learn to demonstrate more empathy with the voter, then Mmusi needs to learn to emote more strongly on key national issues. He is likeable, but also forgettable. And that is not a good thing in politics. Still, in a party that is tone deaf, Mmusi's communicative strengths are instructive. Of course, for other leaders to learn from Mmusi's strengths would require them to learn to listen actively, and to become more self-critical.

But active listening and tone deafness, as you can imagine, make for awkward bedfellows.

A final example: Ian Ollis once allowed himself a moment of beautiful rhetorical flourish in 2012 in front of a mainly student crowd at Wits University. After much debate between me and a few DA MPs about the party's shortcomings, Ian made himself vulnerable in his closing statement by telling the story of a lover he once dated. His lover was black, and although the relationship had not lasted, there had been a budding romance. They did not often speak politics, but on one occasion, his black partner confessed to him that to vote for the DA would be impossible because it was, in his lover's opinion, a mainly white party.

Ian concluded, delicately, by saying that his wish is to live in a country where a partner of a different skin colour to his own wouldn't be comfortable making love to him and yet be uncomfortable voting him into public office.

It was profound. Personal. And deeply revealing of just how

personal politics is. I mean, who can sleep 'across the colour bar' but not vote 'across the colour bar'? Is politics *more* personal than sex, even? With that story, Ian showed an understanding of just how personal politics is for black voters in particular. Our lives were rendered political for centuries, so why would two decades of democracy change that lived reality? Ian showed an awareness of our country's headspace. He did not *judge* that headspace. He *observed* it, compassionately, as a reality from which to start his work as a politician. And he told the story in the first person, weaving himself into the story, and taking the risk of bringing the bedroom into the public space. He was humanising politics. He was humanising himself. *He struck the right tone.*

Why is it so hard for DA leaders to realise that this is the way to win the hearts and minds of potential voters?

Even Ian doesn't do that often enough. Ian has a warm presence, and – not unlike Mmusi – a very natural smile. He has open body language and facial expressions that ooze sincerity when he communicates. But Ian doesn't speak personal narrative often enough. In that sense, the story he told that day was an unusual communication device for him.

And I don't know why he doesn't use it more often. Stories, as I said at the beginning with my confession about the limits of formal debate, can do wonders to bowl an audience over. Personal stories are instantly believable for the obvious reason that they are real. It is hard to fake sincerity when you are relaying truth. It is harder to come across as giving a damn, however, when you are citing cold facts from a spreadsheet on a slide that is being projected onto a conference wall.

Ian did that pitch perfectly that day. His voice was lowered, he spoke more slowly than usual, and one felt like you were sitting with him on a balcony, just exchanging stories about life in our beloved Mzansi. How often, dear reader, do you feel like THAT when Helen or Lindiwe or Athol speaks?

And that is the crux of the communications weakness of the DA.

The sooner the party learns how to communicate effectively, the better. Till then, it will struggle to convert the black UCT graduate unsure of her job prospects; it will struggle to convert Simphiwe Dana; and it will struggle to convert many of us who not only want a party that has smart policies and competent staff but also a party that demonstrates humanity in the way it communicates. A demanding list? Sure. But I have no historic loyalty to the DA so I can afford to be demanding.

Sorry, DA.

4

GANA: THE WRONG KIND OF BLACK?

Is diverse black talent nurtured in the DA?

Why is Gana invisible while Maimane and Mazibuko are so prominent?

Is it easier to succeed in the DA if you're black middle class rather than black working class?

'm not only fascinated by what parties have to offer the country should they come into power. I'm also fascinated by what a party has to offer those of us who might want to join it and become career politicians. The internal dynamics, opportunities and organisational culture of a political party can help us decide whether or not we want to give it a chance to govern.

And so I have been wondering about the career prospects of young black people who join the DA. After all, how the DA engages young black people inside the party might help me decide whether or not the party has the right attitude and programmes to help develop this economically excluded group outside of the party.

It's clear that the DA has young black leaders, some of them in very prominent positions. In particular, Lindiwe Mazibuko and Mmusi Maimane. But what's interesting is that these two are both middle class and have learned the grammar of whiteness extremely well, like many of us who went to former Model

C schools, or English-speaking, liberal, formerly whites-only universities.

What makes it easy for you to succeed in corporate South Africa, for example, is if you speak the same cultural or class language, as it were, as the traditional leadership of a company. That's why, if two black candidates are technically exactly the same, but one sounds like the CEO's son, and the other like the CEO's driver, it is the one mimicking his son who will get the job. In other words, black middle-class employees are safe for some companies to take a chance on. It's harder to know where to slot working-class black South Africans into your organisation.

I think the same applies to the DA as a political party. I want to tell the story of Makashule Gana, who has been in the DA for a very long time, and yet he hasn't been fast-tracked like Mmusi and Lindiwe. Could it be because of his working-class background?

You definitely know Lindiwe Mazibuko. You probably know Mmusi Maimane. You might know Mbali Ntuli. I bet my healthy left kidney very few of you have ever heard of Makashule Gana.

One reason for this hierarchy of popularity is seemingly innocent.

Mazibuko is in the most prominent position of the four within the party; she is of course the leader of the official opposition in Parliament. How could she not be famous? Maimane, who loves playing with various titles, is, among others, the national spokesperson of the party, which means constant media exposure.

Ntuli is the federal youth leader, a considerably less public and less important role than those of Mazibuko and Maimane. But Ntuli is a bubbly, articulate and increasingly media-savvy politician. And so chances are you have caught a glimpse of her in a popular magazine while waiting for your doctor.

Her predecessor, however, and her political senior by a gigantic distance, is Gana. He is also currently one of the deputy federal chairpersons of the Democratic Alliance, basically the equivalent of being one of the ANC's top six leaders. A very senior position indeed.

Add to that the fact that Gana was the youth leader for several years, and was in DA structures long before Maimane even dreamed of being on the party's posters as their Gauteng Premier candidate, and you wonder a bit about Gana's relative obscurity despite his seniority among these four.

Gana joined the DA, as I will soon recount, way before brand DA caught on among black students on South African campuses. So why is he, greater among these four young black DA politicians, taking a particularly long time to gain prominence?

The full answer lies, in the first instance, in a comparison: lesser experienced black talent like Mazibuko and Maimane rose to the top in record time. Unlike those two, Gana, to put it bluntly, is not the kind of black person the DA is comfortable to sell to both its traditional voters and to a pool of new voters. He is not the kind of black guy who would appear in one of those DA posters – or, heaven forbid, a video – about a future in which race and stereotypes do not matter. He is, to appropriate the usefully rude word that political analyst Prince Mashele once used in reference to President Jacob Zuma, a 'ruralitarian'.

He is more *ekasi*, and less 'former Model C'. He might scare tannies in Vereeniging who otherwise loooooove Maimane who, by comparison, 'speaks so well!' And he is less well politically groomed than Maimane and Mazibuko.

This raises several issues. Is the DA a place that enables young black talent from different backgrounds to flourish? Or is it a space in which only the likes of Mazibuko and Maimane can flourish? Is the DA comfortable about explicitly offering talented young black kids the equivalent of an affirmative action leadership programme that is specifically tailored to their needs, lived experiences and the lack of social capital that has hamstrung their development elsewhere in society?

This matters to me as a voter for sure. I could not vote for the DA if the DA was unsure whether or not it was comfortable about deliberately nurturing black talent. Not *just* talent. *Black* talent.

But I want more. I want evidence of excellent mentoring and resources well spent to groom those aspiring black politicians who do join the DA.

Let me explain the challenge using a corporate analogy. When I worked at McKinsey & Company, arguably the world's top strategy and management consulting firm, there was a massive problem with hiring black South Africans for the local McKinsey office in Johannesburg. The reason? Black students had poor marks in matric maths, and that alone excluded almost all of their paper applications to the firm. The ones who passed that hurdle then needed to have an average of about 70% for their undergraduate university courses.

Many black South African students did not stand a chance. Even if you got over those academic hurdles, you were expected to have a CV filled with examples of leadership excellence outside the lecture theatre, write a bloody hard maths-based entrance test and – the worst horror of the lot – go through several rounds of case-study interviews in a high-rise building in Sandton with partners from around the world.

What chance does your average kid from Alex or Soweto stand? Almost zero. You could either conclude that black kids are dumb and white kids amazingly smart and hard-working, or you could conclude the obvious truth: structural historical reasons make the McKinsey system of evaluating talent hopelessly unfair. Not just unfair on talented black kids who had little opportunity to excel in under-resourced environments, but also unfair on the Johannesburg office, which struggled to gain access to government work because it couldn't attract enough black employees.

The moral of the corporate example is this: McKinsey took a long, historical view and finally *found* talented black kids by interrogating their own criteria. This is not the same as the racist assumption that one must 'drop standards'. But you might realise that a 'B' for maths in a poor school is more impressive than an 'A' from St John's, for example. So currently, McKinsey has a talent programme specifically aimed at black students.

They nurture them, and then they feed into the main consulting work of the firm.

The programme is not a perfect success. But it is practical. It is yielding some clear wins. And the firm ought to be more proud than it seems to be that it embraces a deliberate strategy of nurturing not just talent, but black talent. This is a demonstrable need in South Africa; this is the elephant in the boardroom of corporate South Africa.

Sadly, the DA is unable to explicitly nurture black talent because of its scepticism about affirmative action. It has a much-punted, complex and well-resourced leadership programme for young people. But because the party wants to be colour-blind, it is unable to speak directly, and unashamedly, to young black politicos in particular. In other words, it has to pretend to be a programme based on needs, and inadvertently catch decent numbers of black leaders.

In addition, when it does manage to fast-track black talent, it does so clumsily. Both Maimane and Mazibuko, for example, have been given leadership positions with massive responsibilities but little supportive scaffolding and mentoring. Two conclusions can be drawn from this messy handling of black talent: (a) The DA needs to become comfortable with the possibility of an explicit, black-targeted leadership scheme; and (b) The current black leaders in the party urgently need to be given much better support. The second weakness, I suspect, is related to the first. It is hard to deliberately give Maimane support as a black leader if you pretend his blackness has nothing to do with his fast-tracking.

This failure to speak directly to the challenges facing black talent makes the DA unattractive to many of us. If only the party realised that it would endear itself to us with a more honest assessment of the impact that racism's past has had on young black South Africans. Black voters need an alternative to the ANC that starts from a place of historical honesty. Right now the stories of the black leaders in the DA demonstrate the party's clumsy handling of apartheid's reach into the new South Africa.

MAKASHULE GANA: A CASE STUDY OF WHY THE DA NEEDS A BLACK LEADERSHIP PROGRAMME

Makashule was born on the 11th of August 1983 in Lefara Village in Tzaneen, an area that was under the chieftancy of one Mhlaba II. He attended several schools in the village before eventually finishing Grades 10 to 12 as a boarder at a high school in Giyani.

He is the second of three children raised by a single mother. Mom was a cleaner before later becoming a 'general worker' for the Department of Agriculture. The young Makashule was a herd boy looking after goats and cattle. But do not be fooled by the mention of animals: this was – and in many ways still is – a dirt-poor village.

The village was only supplied with electricity in 2010. Very

few households had access to water. In fact – and Gana's comfort with numbers and dates give a hint in interviews of his raw
academic acumen that eventually saw him escape poverty – he
remembers 1995 as the last year he saw water coming out of his
tap. The rest of the time water had to be fetched with a wheelbar-
row from a communal supply point for the village. When that
source ran dry, Gana found himself walking to the next village
in search of water.

A strange observation from Gana stuck with me. He has a
distinct memory of how unremarkable the poverty of his child-
hood was. The reason? Poverty was the norm. There was no inequality. You might say that poverty was an equal-opportunity
bastard. And so there was little resentment of neighbours, and
little need to feel like the loser family. Out of about 250 families,
for example, only six had television sets – and most of these
were cranky old black-and-white things.

It was at boarding school that the talented Gana got a whiff
of life away from the village. It is also here that he was to learn
a sense of independence, a sense of individuality. And, in a
very real way, this would become the earliest foundations of his
buy-in to the DA's liberal individualism. Gana's life was, from
a young age, about going against the social grain – against the
village narrative of poverty – forging his own path. Gana had
no hesitation about joining a liberal party.

Gana's life experiences, despite being very different to
those of the stereotypical middle-class white person – a more
natural poster child for the DA – were the basis of his path to

championing a political ideology that prioritised individualism over the family and society.

In 2000 he enrolled at Turfloop (a campus of the University of Limpopo), and there his political activism started a week after registration. He saw students with ANC, SASCO (South African Students' Congress) and SACP (South African Communist Party) logos on their T-shirts. He was drawn to them and decided to join SASCO. He did this despite not quite understanding at the time exactly what these student political bodies stood for (other than being against 7% fee increases and wanting the vice-chancellor to be fired).

Gana's enthusiasm paid off. In 2001 he was elected to the desk of information publicity in SASCO. This competed for his attention with the BSc in Mathematics and Computer Science for which he was enrolled and which he duly completed.

But by 2001 he had started drifting politically. He was clear in our conversations that he was independent-minded and was bothered by the lack of clarity around what exactly was driving many of the students' political platforms. Like the closet liberal individualist that he was, he did not want to be defined by the environment from which he came.

And so he contested the SRC (Student Representative Council) election as an independent. Nationally, the politics of the ANC turned him off – he recalls the blemish of the arms deal engulfing the presidency of Thabo Mbeki. Then, empowered by his sense of independence on campus, he questioned why he still wanted to be an ANC member and could find no satisfactory answer given the trouble that brand ANC, in his assessment, was in.

It was now just a matter of finding a new political home, and so he started looking around. The Pan Africanist Congress, in light of their ever dwindling numbers, seemed to be a 'dying party'. He was suspicious of the United Democratic Movement's (UDM) prospects after the exit of Roelf Meyer. He concluded that the UDM would then be precariously built around an individual.

That left, realistically, the IFP (Inkatha Freedom Party) and the DA. For better or worse Gana thought that the IFP was more of a Zulu thing and he feared that Zulus did not like Shangaans like him. He started following the DA very closely. He watched *Parliament Live* on TV and the DA's relentless opposition performance attracted him to the party. He recalled being enthralled by Douglas Gibson engaging Mbeki, for example, on Zimbabwean farm invasions.

He went to the DA's website and found it informative and up to date. He familiarised himself with the DA and became convinced that it was a good party with lots of opportunities.

He sent an email to the DA. The party responded. It sent his details to the provincial leader in Limpopo who gave him a call. That was 2002. They set up a meeting with a local DA leader, and she brought a form. He signed it, gave them R10, and that is how his journey with the DA began. Soon he would serve on youth structures and in 2003 became the provincial chairperson of the DA Student Organisation in Limpopo, eventually moving to Johannesburg where he was to become the federal youth leader and, these days, both a deputy federal chairperson of the main body of the party, and a local councillor in Johannesburg.

It sounds well and good, but there are several aspects of Gana's story that show just how bad the DA is at attracting *and developing* a diverse pool of talented black leaders, especially among the youth.

First, there is a failure to understand that Gana's story is far more recognisable to most black South Africans than Mazibuko's. Gana's story is a typical South African story of poverty, lucky opportunity (which is probably not typical) and an abiding awareness of one's humble beginnings. Mazibuko, by contrast, is an almost-born free who accessed good educational and social opportunities at an early stage.

Some speak very disparagingly about him. A senior MP even called him, off the record, a moron. The irony is that on some issues Gana is more thoughtful than the MP who hurled this private insult at him. But the MP is white, English-speaking, fluent, extroverted and deems Gana, who is none of those things, the epitome of a talentless black person who has support from a 'sponsoring' senior white person.

This does not mean Mazibuko must bemoan not growing up dirt poor. Or, worse, be ashamed of her educational excellence, and social class. But the party, by failing to take Gana as seriously as Maimane and Mazibuko, just because he does not speak fluent

English and has the social awkwardness that comes with his background, demonstrates an inability to talk to the majority of black South Africans. If I only ever read the *Sowetan* and never picked up *Business Day*, I would need a particularly special reason to see myself reflected in the leadership of Mazibuko and Maimane.

Gana's biography clearly has more appeal. So why is it not propelled into the public space? The reason is simple: most of the senior leaders in the DA are not comfortable enough about deliberately looking for, and developing, talent among poor black South Africans.

Sure, if you look at pictures of a DA rally these days, the numbers of black Africans have increased steadily. In fact, at many DA events blacks are in the majority even. But recall that we are talking here about whether or not, as a voter unsure about the DA, I would take a chance on the party. And it seems to me that one unnecessary obstacle the DA has created for itself is not being a comfortable space in which a certain kind of black person can easily rise to the top.

I probably could – I speak fairly well, have travelled the world, won debate and public-speaking competitions, and can give Mazibuko a run for her debating money. But what about my coloured sibling and cousins? What about Makashule Gana? Despite his ambition – which he shared with me – of wanting to lead both his party and our country, the truth is that right now he has hit a glass ceiling. That ceiling is because *he is not the right-sounding black leader* to be punted by a majority of senior peers in the party.

That is the subtext that develops in a party that is unable to bluntly, and unashamedly, develop black talent. Thus, the talent is left to its own devices, and becomes the subject of gossip and whispering campaigns.

This brings us back to the voter. Why would a voter, filled with uncertainty about the DA's sincerity to develop them, easily vote for the DA in the face of what they know about Gana who has been in the party for more than ten years and is still looking and sounding lost in the eyes of his political peers? The DA is not sending the right signals to those voters who do not fit the profile of the imagined DA voter. And the party is to blame for that. It is the result of their failure of imagination, their failure to embrace a race-based affirmative action leadership programme for talented black South Africans.

The second point that shows how bad the DA is at attracting *and developing* diverse black leaders is that Gana needs help. When I first asked him whether the DA was a liberal party, for example, he could not answer. A few weeks later, to his credit, he came back to a later interview with a more certain answer: that indeed, the party was liberal and he himself was a liberal. He then explained his liberalism, not in terms of political theory (which is totally fine of course), but in terms of his sense of individualism as a child and as a student at Turfloop. He was clear. Yes, family and society matter, but only when the individual chooses to opt into these social structures. This is why he hates communal land-ownership solutions to the land-redistribution challenge, for example. He thinks communal ownership stifles the individual's economic freedom to decide how they want to exploit their portion of land.

This was a decent, humble and practical way of explaining what being committed to liberal individualism means for him. But the bottom line is that Gana is out of his depth when he is engaged on political ideology and policy. The first time we had this chat he suggested that the word 'liberal' did not appear in any official DA document! Helen Suzman – bless her – must have turned in her liberal grave.

Equally, on policy matters I struggled to find in Gana evidence of a politician who had been in the party for ten years. He casually asserted that the DA was in favour of Black Economic Empowerment, specifically designed in terms of race rather than some other criterion like need or class. But when I pointed out that other leaders have critiqued BEE, and some have called for race-based redress to be ditched, he was unable to nimbly state the party's official position, clearly, and then locate himself and disagreeing colleagues on the same policy map.

Most embarrassingly of all, he could not find the official party position on BEE so that we could go through it together to see if he was right or whether his colleagues who disagree with him were right.

But perhaps Gana's biggest weakness is that he is a tragically poor communicator. This brings us back to the DA's clumsy engagement with voters who want to see evidence of empathetic engagement with non-traditional supporters of the party. If I am a black voter who is as uncomfortable in the English language as Gana, and see that he has not been sufficiently developed within the party despite being there for ten years, why would I believe that the party really cares about black people? If it did, why has it not by now found a coach to help Gana with his communication weaknesses, and taught him how to easily explain the party's main ideological foundations and key policy proposals? In fact, given that Gana is one of the party's deputy federal chairpersons, I cannot help but wonder what he is doing in such a senior position despite such demonstrable political and technical weaknesses?

And, as a prevaricating voter not already married to the DA, I might be tempted to think the worst. Is the DA fronting? Is the DA happy to say that it has a rural man from Limpopo as a deputy federal chairperson *even though the party's most senior leaders do not actually respect him?*

Not only is this patronising Gana – and grossly unfair to him – but it also patronises black voters. The unspoken assumption is that a mere change in the colour of the leadership will gain traction among voters.

In reality, a well-resourced, well-thought-through programme of leadership training and development, aimed at attracting and nurturing black talent is what would do the trick. And then show off a brilliant Gana who clearly, after ten years, has been groomed, mentored and developed.

Sadly, the DA does not have such a targeted programme. And it cannot. Why? Because it insists on not seeing black and white, even though voters actually do. For better or worse. The party needs to start living in the country in which it is canvassing votes. And not in the one it wished it lived in.

The bottom line with Gana is simple: if Gana had the exact same qualifications, skills and life experiences, but he were white and perhaps his name was Piet Erasmus, he would not be the deputy federal chairperson. Of that, I am dead certain. So why give underdeveloped black talent discount for their gross developmental weaknesses?

Not only is this ironic – because you have to see Gana as black to let him off the hook (which many in the DA pretend they do not see, what with the colour-blind motif being so popular) – but, furthermore, it does not endear the party to black voters who are not middle class and who do not look and sound like Mazibuko or Maimane. For these voters, taking a chance on the DA becomes a massive gamble. The DA could remedy this by showing an ability to love a Gana as much as a Mazibuko. But that requires rethinking their programme and the expenditure of resources. It is not obvious to me that the DA is likely to be that honest about the context within which it exists anytime soon.

THE FALSE EXCEPTIONALISM OF ELOQUENT BLACKS

It is not just someone like Gana, however, who is not sufficiently groomed for leadership positions he is not ready for. Throughout this chapter I have, unintentionally, conveyed the impression of excellence on the part of Maimane and Mazibuko.

The truth, however, is that these young black leaders are equally the victims of the DA's failure to think through an explicit development and mentoring programme. It is just that we live in a country where there is, as writer Jonny Steinberg once said, 'an anthropology of low expectations'. Mazibuko and Maimane, in different ways, are both very eloquent communicators, confident politicians and socially savvy people, apparently able to negotiate their public roles with intimidating excellence.

But pay attention to the details of how their careers are playing out in the DA and it is clear that all is not well. Take Maimane. He has been, so far, Premier candidate for the DA in Gauteng, caucus leader of the DA councillors in Johannesburg, deputy federal chairperson of the party and simultaneously the national spokesperson. It was only a temporary crisis of confidence that stopped him in 2012 from running for the top party provincial leadership position in Gauteng.

This is not admirable. This is the patchy job-hopping CV of a young politician who is not adequately mentored to patiently earn his right to occupy a senior position by gaining either governance experience within the council, properly, and/or slowly building a deep network of credible relationships at grassroots level, in a bottom-up manner within the party's structures.

Why the rush, therefore, from leaders like Helen Zille to use their suasion to ensure he gets elected easily into a senior position? Simple. He is black. As with Gana, it is unavoidable to conclude that but for the fact that Maimane is black, some of these leadership positions would not yet be on his political CV.

Even with his excellent professional and academic credentials it is obvious that Maimane is out of his depth as a caucus leader on the Johannesburg council. Speak to a critical number of councillors off the record and this becomes apparent. So it raises the question: what explains his amazing trajectory? And, more importantly, is this trajectory in Maimane's own interest? Is it in the party's interest? And what does it say to us voters who wonder what it means to be a talented, but underprepared, black person entering the DA?

Sadly for the DA, the answers cannot be flattering. Despite the colour-blind rhetoric, Maimane's lack of experience of all things governance did not get in the way of him being the Premier candidate for Gauteng. Maimane's white doppelgänger would never have made it past the internal selection structures of the DA. He was propped up, looks pretty, has a charming smile, speaks beaaaaaautifully, so why not put him on posters around Gauteng?

Two horrible consequences follow: (a) Maimane's professional development gets retarded (because the party then has to pretend he is already fit for purpose and so does not offer him the necessary scaffolding to learn); and (b) it sends the message to black voters that the DA loves cosmetics, but not necessarily well-thought-through processes to harness black people with potential. Some DA members even tell me that in a crude, if unintended, way Maimane was set up to fail because of this hasty shoving into positions he had not earned.

This is not the way to attract, nurture and develop talent. It is patronising. And it shows a lack of sincere interest in dealing with the racial legacy of the country by intervening more thoughtfully in the lives of black people. Maimane might be comfortable in the media space now, but he is in reality too weak for the position of deputy federal chair. It is little wonder, for example, as I narrated in an earlier chapter, that Van Onselen was able to have Maimane for breakfast, publicly, in a debate about liberalism and Ubuntu.

The party lets down not just ruralitarians like Gana but also former Model C talents like Mazibuko and Maimane.

* * *

Is all lost for the party? Not at all. But it will take uncharacteristic political balls for the DA to admit that: (a) blacks and whites actually exist; (b) black talent needs specific attention; (c) it needs to design a more thoughtful programme for developing black talent comprehensively; and, perhaps the most difficult of all (d) it must accept that a longer time frame is needed before you can unveil to the media the first black leader of the opposition or your first black Premier candidate. Haste leads to cosmetic choices that convey a message of clumsy and patronising engagement with black South Africans' reality.

It is up to the DA to re-engage many voters' concerns about its approach to the lived realities of those who might vote DA but do not feel like the party 'gets' them. A good start is not to set up the young, gifted and black for failure and ridicule in the secret gaze of their experienced white peers. The uncertain voter is watching you.

5

DA LIES ABOUT BEE

Is the **DA** genuinely committed to **BEE**?

Is it better to focus on diversity rather than race in policy language?

Why is the **DA** divided on this policy?

There's always a debate around election times about whether or not policies matter to voters. It is in principle a reasonably easy question to settle; someone should come and ask us as voters. But unfortunately opinion polling isn't a well-established science in South Africa so we often – analysts included – simply guess what does and doesn't matter.

This presented me with a dilemma – how many chapters on policy questions do I include in a book about whether or not I could vote DA? And, actually, I wasn't sure. The strange thing is that good policies, properly implemented, can improve all of our lives. So you'd think that policies would obviously matter to all of us.

But reality is trickier. For example, although I could wax lyrical about the details of ANC policies – which bits I like, which bits I think need rethinking – the truth is that, for me, the ANC's weakness in government has not fundamentally been a lack of good policy ideas. It has been a governance challenge. It has simply not been able to successfully see through to implementation all of the good policy frameworks they have established.

And so I'd happily vote, for example, for a political party that can convince me that they have the men and women with the necessary skill and political will to better implement the ANC's policies.

This is only a slight exaggeration. One can, for example, quibble about whether the welfare state is properly designed under the ANC's watch or whether the housing policy has been the best for allowing access to settlements that can restore people's dignities, etc.

But, really, the bigger reason why we're not an even better society than we might otherwise have been after almost twenty years of democracy, is because of practical, governance weaknesses, not policy ones.

And so I am not sure, actually, whether radically different policy proposals from the DA, next to those currently in place from the ANC, will be the ultimate determinant of whether or not I will vote DA. I doubt that.

This makes it hard for the DA in that it either has to convince me to care deeply about some genuine alternative policy ideas the party has, or alternatively the DA must appeal to other things that also matter to voters.

For this reason I didn't think it would be appropriate to do a comprehensive assessment here of every single major DA policy. Doing so would amount to a lie about how much weight

I am going to actually place on policy differentiation when I decide who to vote for. Truth be told, it is very hard to find sharp ideological differences between the ANC and DA in the policy domain.

And that's why, by the way, I devote so much space to things that the DA often assumes are less important, but actually are the things that can make us fall in and out of love with a political party, such as who the men and women in leadership positions are or whether or not we like the way the party speaks to us, and engages us.

There is one policy discussion, however, that ignites our passions, mine included. It is Black Economic Empowerment. I've seen this every time I have initiated a public debate on BEE, be it in a newspaper, on social media platforms, or on radio. And every time I interview politicians about their views on BEE, on my radio show the phone lines are jammed with reactions from the public; more so than with any other policy issue in the country, including policy debates about economic growth, inequality, crime, etc.

And the DA knows this. Which is why it made a big deal out of a massive billboard it unveiled in late 2013 about BEE, and its view on BEE. The party knew it would be a crucial part of the election campaign, to clarify to black voters in particular, what exactly the party thinks about BEE.

And, sadly, the party has messed up its communications on BEE and probably in the process exposed itself as not really being deeply committed to BEE. That, I must confess, is a huge turn-off, certainly for someone like me who is obsessed with social justice. This is not to say that BEE is the only, or even an effective, answer to the social justice challenge.

Hell, no. BEE has been abused too badly for me to be its champion. But, as I will shortly demonstrate, in the course of making a number of communication errors, the DA revealed to me, as a voter who cares about redress for racial injustice, that this is one debate where the party really doesn't have a clue.

Here's what happened …

MAIMANE VS JAMES: WHO TO BELIEVE?

So the DA unveils a massive billboard in Joburg that says, 'We support BEE that creates jobs, not billionaires.' This was launched with huge fanfare as the second phase of the 'Know Your DA' campaign.

I don't know who the DA thought it was fooling with this slogan. The reference to BEE in that message is meaningless. What the billboard should simply have said, more honestly, is something like 'We support job creation'. Or, perhaps, 'We oppose the results of BEE thus far'. Because all the billboard tells me is that the party wants us all to have jobs, and thinks it is uncool if only a few people become billionaires.

And you know what? I agree! Duhuh. What right-minded,

socially conscious voter would disagree with a party that says it has a dream that we should create jobs, and another dream that not just a few people should become wealthy.

But say that without pretending that those two dreams amount to an endorsement of BEE.

BEE is an independent set of policy interventions in the economy to transfer wealth and economic opportunities into black hands, *in addition to other policies aimed at job creation and economic growth.*

So it is a complete and utter red herring to talk about job creation, economic growth and BEE in the same breath. Put it this way: you and I can agree on the importance of, and strategies for, job creation and economic growth, and yet end up in disagreement about BEE specifically.

So I was immediately suspicious, as one of those voters who has a keen passion for the BEE debate, when I saw this slogan. It made me feel as if the DA was trying to pull a fast one on me. It made me feel the party hoped I would simply now regard it as a champion of BEE, just because it was keen on job creation, and not keen on billionaires.

But I'm afraid I am wide awake on this one, because BEE – for reasons I will still come to – is a topic to which I pay close attention.

Unsettled by the clumsily worded billboard and with lingering suspicions of disingenuousness on the part of the DA, I decided to invite the party onto my radio show to explain its stance to the public, and for all of us to debate the DA's policy position on BEE. It turned out to be a fascinating exercise.

It was Wilmot James, the DA's federal chairperson, who represented the party. All started well with him explaining that the list of things for which companies get BEE points – these points being useful, if you don't know it, in ensuring you get tenders from the state – must be bigger than the current list of things for which you get BEE points.

In other words, they weren't looking to scrap the codes so much as expand them in order, hopefully, to be more effective in ensuring even broader-based Black Economic Empowerment.

And so, for example, companies might now get BEE points for job creation, diversity, etc.

This in itself isn't inherently a bad idea. If you want to incentivise companies to do socially useful things with a points-reward system, then fine. That can only help us, I guess.

I do, as an aside, think that an expansion of the codes is unnecessary. It is the point of other government policies to unlock job opportunities, skills development opportunities, etc. And so it seems clumsy to basically chuck the objectives of a raft of other policies into the BEE codes.

But put that aside for now. What really set the phone lines blazing was the final part of my interview with Wilmot.

I asked him how he squares the DA's commitment to non-racialism, which I take to mean a world in which we do not refer to racial categories, with a policy like BEE that is explicitly based on racial categories.

He told me I was right, that the DA isn't into 'racial bean-counting', and that if the DA won the 2014 elections, it would immediately change the BEE policies to remove references to race. Instead, it would refer to diversity rather than race, and it would be up to companies, further, to think through how to achieve diversity in the workplace. In other words, 'Diversity Economic Empowerment' rather than Black Economic Empowerment.

Wilmot agreed with this language change for the policy he actually wants. So, the DA wasn't into BEE after all. Wilmot was honest.

Why pretend you're into BEE when you're actually colour-blind? That means the billboard, as I suspected, was a lie. And many of the listeners of my show expressed a similar sentiment. But what was most fascinating about their reaction was the intensity with which they explained how much they had been looking forward to clarity on the DA's position on BEE. And now they had got clarity from Wilmot: he was insincere in initially saying he supported BEE, only later to reveal his true, colourless self.

This wouldn't be a big deal for the DA if it wasn't for the fact that BEE, like I said, is one policy area that many of us care deeply about. If you wonder why, by the way, it is for the breathtakingly simple reason that – putting aside implementation bungles for the moment – blacks were deliberately and systematically excluded from economic opportunities during apartheid, and BEE policies aim to address that legacy.

We have achieved political freedom, but we certainly remain a substantively unequal society. And in BEE, rightly or wrongly, many of us recognise the need to deliberately disrupt an unjust economic status quo born of a racist apartheid past.

I want to be absolutely clear that this does not mean I am endorsing the abuse of BEE. BEE has been a right mess in practice. But here's the crucial bit: Wilmot made the mistake of not being able to separate a conversation about economic justice, based on racial inequalities, from a very different conversation about BEE's practical shortcomings.

He shot himself in the foot by unnecessarily using the failure of BEE to go the extra mile and undermine racial categories in a country in which many of us still experience poverty and exclusion along racial lines.

His disastrous interview was a gift to the ANC. He should have restricted himself to a simple, familiar, empirical critique of BEE as a policy that does not benefit the black African masses in our country. That would have been easy and, frankly, bang on the money.

But no, he overstated his case, in a fatal way, coming across like a politician who is blind to the need for specific interventions to undo the impact of racial inequality. The evidence of this mistake was his unnecessary obsession with 'diversity' rather than economic justice for black people.

That is not just ahistoricism of the worst kind; it is also politically a huge mistake. I want a party to tell me that they are sick and tired, yes, of a few billionaires benefiting from BEE (or even its pointless reinvention, BBBEE – Broad-Based Black Economic Empowerment). But I do not want that party to use this diagnosis as an excuse to deny my race-specific experiences of exclusion.

And that's why my radio callers, in my view, turned on Wilmot. They are not naïve about BEE's abuse. But Wilmot left a bad taste in their mouths with his clumsily stated view about race categories being so last-year.

Now I have no doubt many supporters of the DA – especially the traditional white support base – will think Wilmot was on point. But let me remind you, you already vote DA, and the question is how the DA can grow beyond you. I'm afraid it cannot grow without locating itself in my headspace, rather than affirming yours as correct and normative.

Mmusi Maimane knows this. And that's why he, as a fellow DA leader, was outraged by Wilmot's own goal in that interview. Mmusi immediately went on a media blitz in the following 24 hours to undo the damage.

Mmusi made it clear to me that the DA is absolutely committed to colour-coded policy language on this issue. It wasn't about diversity, he assured me. It was, bluntly, about black Africans in particular enjoying economic justice. In other words, it was not the 'diversity' Wilmot had said it was about.

So who does one believe? Wilmot or Mmusi? Frankly, I think I am confused as a voter! It didn't help that senior white DA leaders were noticeably silent. They shout like a choir ensemble on other topics, like the e-toll saga. Yet on this topic, Mmusi was a lone Africanist voice trying to drown out Wilmot's damaging narrative about BEE.

And how did I feel about the party's handling of this? For one thing, the lack of overt support from the entire leadership of the DA, especially senior white leaders, made me suspect that this policy is not sincerely, and wholly, endorsed by the DA's leadership.

And, given how much I care about this particular policy, it left me disappointed. Here was a chance for the party to edge closer to my heart, my headspace, as a prevaricating voter open to falling in love with the DA. And all they did with this disunity and silence from some was cement my suspicion that they really do not share my views on economic injustice and race; that they had simply hoped to pull a fast one with a slogan on a billboard.

I'm sorry, but my vote is not that cheap.

For another, I thought that the party had chosen Mmusi and Lindiwe as the face of this billboard rollout because they actually thought black leaders could persuade a black voter they were serious about BEE, and so the whites were again told to stay in the background on this one, just as the white men who played important roles in the party were absent from that first video released about the party's history (an issue I tackle in the next chapter).

My suspicions were confirmed by one of the federal executive leaders of the party who told me that, indeed, it was decided that Helen Zille should not be spearheading an explanation of the party's position on BEE. I was also told that Wilmot didn't agree with the policy position adopted, which was why he went off-message so quickly after I pressured him into explaining the apparent clash between BEE and non-racialism.

Wilmot could not play ball, this leader said, because Wilmot did not buy the arguments for BEE, but had lost the debate inside the party. What baffles me, though, is why on earth the DA would put forward for a key interview on BEE a person who didn't actually believe the party was doing the right thing? No wonder Wilmot didn't stick to the script.

But the consequence of this entire saga is simple. I just do not trust the sincerity of the DA's commitment to Black Economic Empowerment. Wilmot's off-message words are closer to the views of most DA leaders I have privately engaged on race-based policies in general. Mmusi's view, closer to mine, is less common within the DA.

And so it is clear that the billboard was an election ploy, rather than the result of some amazing dialectic inside the party that ended in a deep and sincere, intellectual and political commitment to race-based redress policies like BEE.

What reinforced this conviction in me, by the way, is that Mmusi himself had rejected racial categories in policy language in an interview with me several weeks before! And I have the recording to prove it. Before the DA unveiled this billboard I had had Mmusi on my show to talk about this policy issue and in the course of that conversation, he too, like Wilmot, shifted the focus from race to socio-economic need and diversity talk.

I reminded Mmusi of that interview when he tried to persuade me that Wilmot's views weren't the party's view. But he just chuckled, probably hoping I would agree to forget. But of course I can't, neither as a voter nor as an analyst.

That earlier interview with Mmusi meant that he, magically, came round to BEE, in all its racial glory, within the space of a few weeks. So although Mmusi now came across as disagreeing with Wilmot, the deeper truth was that Wilmot's colour-blindness had been echoed by Mmusi himself, on the same platform, some few weeks before!

If not, I don't blame him. This has been a story of DA vagueness, flip-flopping, disunity and insincere sloganeering on one of the most crucial policy debates in our country.

And that is so unfortunate for the DA. Why? 'Cause BEE is bloody easy to diss, and it is easy to curry favour with the masses with an accurate critique of BEE. Instead, the DA messed it up by overstating their problem with BEE, and in the processes revealing their obsession with colour-blindness, in a country where race still plays a powerful role in our daily lives.

I can't say I'm impressed with the DA on the thorny issue of BEE. The party has work to do to convince me I, uhm, 'took them out of context'. And time is running out.

6

HOW NOT TO
PLAY THE ANC

Was the 'Know Your DA' campaign a success?

Does the DA misunderstand the ANC voter's loyalty?

Is it the DA or the ANC voter who needs to change?

I sn't it amazing how family bonds can make us behave in ways that seem inconsistent or hypocritical? I think, for example, of so many aunties in my township in Grahamstown who fight any neighbour who dares talk 'nonsense' about their alcoholic son.

But then, a few hours later, after fighting the gossipmonger, the very same mother who was hellbent on protecting her drunk son's reputation can suddenly be heard shouting at said drunk son, and chasing him out of her house.

'Kevin, *jou dronkgat! VOETSEK! Vat jou goed en TREK!*' ['Kevin, you drunkard! Voetsek! Take your things and GO!'] I can remember these scenes like they were yesterday. If it happened in your home, you'd be helluva embarrassed by the commotion.

But of course if it happened next door, you'd run outside to watch the spectacle, which we kids used to call 'free bioscope'. Ah, how I miss free bioscope. None of that in my boring apartment building now. Wait, it did happen once in my apartment building, but I didn't run outside to watch. The rules seem different here.

Many ANC voters are a bit like protective aunties who do not want their drunk son – called ANC – to be scolded by the neighbours. They hate it! But they reserve the right to scold the ANC themselves.

It's strange, isn't it, and yet strangely *familiar* in other aspects of all our lives. When you love a thing, or a person, you have that kind of complex relationship with it/them. So, for the ANC voter who has had a lifelong love of the party, but who is now disappointed in aspects of ANC government, it touches a raw nerve when outsiders – call them DA leaders – lash out at the ANC.

For these ANC voters, it is as painful as hearing a neighbour gossip truths about your drunk son, or your drunk uncle. Only YOU are allowed to chastise the useless kid in the family, not the outside world.

I seriously think this is one of the facts of political life, and life in general, frankly, that too many in the DA just do not get, particularly when it comes to ANC voters. The way in which the DA engages the ANC's record in government and the ANC's other demonstrable political flaws, shows a failure to consider how the message, and the tone with which it is delivered, will be received by an ANC supporter who secretly agrees with the content of the message.

And that is what this chapter is ultimately about: explaining the strategic communication errors that the DA makes because it hasn't learned to accept that ANC voters want you to engage their first love, their MaKhumalo, the ANC, in a way that doesn't torture the bonds they have with the ANC.

This demand by the ANC voter doesn't mean that the voter is irrational, or beyond the DA's reach. It does, however, mean that the DA must be a helluva lot more savvy in how it engages the ANC if it wishes to tap into the dissatisfaction many ANC voters have with their first political love.

Just as, if I want my neighbour, who is my best friend, to stop letting her life be ruined by her drunkard son, I may have to take her out to Spur one day, laugh and reminisce about the good times, and finally gently lower my voice as I ask, '*Kan ons oor Kevin gesels, tjommie?*' ['Can we talk about Kevin, friend?']

No doubt it is annoying having to take on the ANC. Here is a political party that makes many mistakes. And yet it is not being punished for them as much as you might expect. For starters, the big picture is not very flattering. I have said this before in this book. We are one of the most unequal nations in the Milky Way ... blah blah blah ... We have depressing levels of poverty around the country and of course unemployment is a disaster that refuses to go away with figures as high as 70% if you segment the population to exclude older folk and concentrate on the restless young people whose unemployed energies, by the way, are spent being antisocial, or idle.

But if that is the case, you might think, why the bloody

hell is this stupid party that is not delivering to black people in particular being returned to office with more than 60% of the vote in general elections? MORE THAN BLOODY 60% OF THE VOTE? After that, you might go on to think, WHY ARE VOTERS SO BLOODY STUPID?!!!

And that, in a nutshell, is the problem right there with the DA's take on the voter's relationship with the ANC. That last response is the dominant sentiment I encounter when I speak to DA leaders and DA supporters.

And because the DA can't fathom why millions of people vote for the ANC, the DA in turn comes up with embarrassingly clumsy *responses* to the ANC on a daily basis. This despite the fact that the DA spends lots of money and time and human resources thinking about communications 'strategically'.

It just gets it wrong time and time again.

First, the DA just does not understand the world in which the ANC voter lives. But it also makes the mistake of thinking it can contest liberation history. The ANC, I'm afraid, has a monopoly on that part of our history and the 'Know Your DA' campaign, as former party leader Tony Leon has rightly pointed out, is a mistake.

What would happen to DA communication if the DA thought of the supporter as a rational, complex, fussy creature? Well, for a start, it would be a whole lot more successful. But first, let's try to understand a little better the ANC voters' relationship with their own party.

WHY DO ANC SUPPORTERS SEEM SO LOYAL TOWARDS AN IMPERFECT PARTY?

It's very easy to be deeply puzzled by the relationship between millions of black South Africans and the ANC. But this is really unnecessary.

Let me make a pseudo-concession first before hitting the deep puzzle out of the park. There is *some* stuff that is puzzling about *some* ANC voters. Sure.

Like, if a community protests against the local ANC municipality, burns tyres, destroys community property, etc., then we are right to wonder why on earth they voted a couple of months back for this particular council when they would have known from past experience that the prospects of their service delivery needs being met were minimal.

But there is no deep puzzle here. If you think for more than three seconds with your supposedly superior middle-class brain, then you can actually figure out what is going on here in a way that does not require you to conclude that poor people are irrational.

For one thing, service delivery protests, to unpack this familiar example a bit more, can be seen as a way of expressing discontent about just that – poor service delivery. It is a demand for political accountability. Is it effective or desirable? Not necessarily.

But just because a community resorts to service delivery protests to express their dissatisfaction with a council does not mean that community doesn't have other considerations that shape its decision to return that council to power.

The logic for a protest is very different to the motivation behind voting choices. At the point at which I protest I could, for example, be *gatvol* about the lack of repair work promised on incomplete RDP houses in my neighbourhood and have had enough of unkept promises.

In other words, a very specific set of grievances – sometimes even one solitary grievance not dealt with properly over a long period of time – can ignite the anger of a community and set in motion a protest. That invariably happens between elections.

But now recall the moods of our elections. Voters in our country are not violent at election times. We are calm, often even jovial, and we have the luxury, because of this mood shift, of then taking a longer view of our, uhm, very short post-democratic history than the view we might take when being pissed off with the mayor between elections.

And so, as we reflect calmly about an election, we do not obsess about the *particular* disappointment of one housing project that was messed up by the ANC government in our area. We measure all of the socio-economic conditions in our areas currently against what they were, in our memories, during apartheid.

This is the crucial bit the DA just does not get: a poor ANC voter's benchmark against which they measure progress is NOT a middle-class suburb; it is a crappy, dehumanising apartheid township. And here you have to be the most stubborn of political opponents to not concede that for millions of black South Africans life is relatively better now than during apartheid.

But here is the key bit: life is not as good as it could be, or perhaps even as it should be; there are many lost opportunities because of ANC underperformance, corruption, unethical behaviour, etc. That is not, however, the point. The point, from the ANC supporter's view, is that they can sincerely, and RATIONALLY, say to themselves, '*Thiza wam!* At least we have clinics now! De Klerk never gave us clinics! Zuma must just make sure we now get our sugar medication on time. Please, Mr President!'

There is no irrationality here. You may think the voter should demand more from the politician. But that is not a matter of rationality; that is a matter of different yardsticks being used to measure progress in the change of material conditions.

Any DA leader or supporter who insists on simply ascribing irrationality to ANC voters should really disabuse themselves of the idea. It is false. That tendency embarrassingly shows that the person making that accusation does not live with poor people.

If they lived with poor people they would understand why the evaluation of progress, from the viewpoint of someone who was previously completely destitute, is not irrational.

It should be obvious then why there is nothing deeply puzzling about the relationship between the ANC voter and the ANC.

Many poor ANC voters have seen real material improvements in their communities. They demand more improvement, which is why they often protest. But demanding further improvement is compatible with rewarding a political party for progress that has happened so far.

Sadly, this will be news – controversial news, even – for many DA supporters reading this, precisely because of the patronising attitude among many of their supporters and leaders when it comes to making sense of the ANC supporter.

The astonishment that any poor person could possibly have good reason to support the ANC runs so deep that many in the DA end up playing Dr Phil, trying to explain the irrationality of ANC members, rather than simply accepting that poor people can be rational in their choices.

The irony is that the DA would make inroads among these voters more quickly if they treated them as rational rather than as irrational.

There is also a perception, I find, among many in the DA that the ANC voter votes for the ANC because of history. This is misguided for reasons I explore below.

Currently a lot of the DA's communication is completely off the mark precisely because the communication strategist lives in his own world, not the world of the ANC voter he wants to win over. Because the strategist regards the ANC voter as irrational, the strategies are not particularly well thought through. The strategist insists on thinking the ANC voter's identity and sense of history are the overriding, if not the exclusive, basis of her voting for the ANC and so wrongly insists that communication needs to mainly engage *these* issues ahead of 2014.

Clearly, the DA simply does not 'get' the millions of people who vote ANC.

Now let's see what would happen if the DA reversed its assumptions about the ANC voter and supporter.

A useful way of thinking through what this would mean is to look at their misplaced 'Know Your DA' campaign.

DA COMMUNICATIONS MISS THE POINT ...

So, the DA's internal research led it to believe that black voters are madly in love with liberation history. So much so that brand ANC cannot easily be challenged unless the DA somehow convinces the black voter that they also have a proud liberation history.

The logic is simple: 'Blacks are suckers for anti-apartheid nostalgia ... Let's give 'em some!' And thus was born the 'Know Your DA' campaign, a campaign the party, astoundingly, still regarded as a success at the time of writing this chapter. But it was anything but a success. The idea was to tell the true story of the involvement of DA leaders in the fight against apartheid and in shaping our democracy. It launched the campaign by releasing a video that told us about the great Helen Suzman and along the way Helen Zille, the current leader of the party, got a mention too. And those were, uhm, the only white names to make an appearance in the video about the DA's history.

The rest of the individuals featured in the video were black – people like Patricia de Lille, Wilmot James and others.

Conspicuously absent, of course, were the white men who actually are the key voices in the history of the DA and the parties that preceded the DA – men like Tony Leon, Zack de Beer, Frederik van Zyl Slabbert, and many others.

At any rate, the video basically told us the political biographies of the individuals who were featured, and the conclusion drawn was that their combined biographies show that the DA, too, contributed towards the liberation of South Africa from the evil that was apartheid.

And never again will the party let the ANC get away with, in its opinion, distorting the DA's place in history in the consciousness of the public.

So why do I think the campaign was misguided when the party is so chuffed with itself, even with many months having passed and the time for assessing impact and thinking critically about the initiative has come and gone?

First, this campaign patronisingly assumes that black people are slaves to history. It continues to imagine, as I said earlier, that the primary reason why a poor black person votes for the ANC is because she is in the grip of nostalgia.

If the DA did not think so, then why the heck would it be spending so much capital on a risky campaign aimed at competing with the ANC's liberation credentials? The only explanation for taking on such massive political risk is because you think to yourself that history matters to black people, almost as a matter of life and death.

The black voter, yet again, is not allowed to be complex. She is the subject of a simple diagnosis, and the target of an equally simple intervention, just as her reason for voting ANC and also taking part in a service delivery protest can simply be explained as irrationality.

Don't get me wrong: the DA could in theory demonstrate more complex thinking by combining a campaign about history with other campaigns that focus on bread-and-butter issues. But the way in which the actual campaign played out was crude; it insulted the black voter's intelligence.

'What need does the black voter have of being subtly induced to vote for the DA?' seems to be the subtext behind the first video with its airbrushing of white men from DA history. Not only is the black voter treated as a slave to history, but as an uncritical respondent to historical material. A double insult.

The party came up with the most disingenuous defence when confronted with the video's missing men, claiming that everyone already knew the history of these men. What nonsense! I bet you R10 000 that if you stop any twenty black people in DA T-shirts at a DA rally tomorrow and ask them to give you a thirty-second summary of Frederik van Zyl Slabbert and what he did in the fight against apartheid, not more than three or four would give you a decent answer. Fewer, probably, would know about De Beer, and while everyone might recognise Tony Leon as the previous party leader, very few could tell you details about his actual contribution.

And yet these men, actually, are incredibly important South Africans. Tony Leon, for example, whether you love him or hate him, did a hell of a lot to role-model opposition oversight in Parliament by asking critical questions and not being distracted by any moral discomfort that one might have felt on account of being a white politician in the early days of a majority black government.

His name should not only be known; his *role* should be known, and critically debated and discussed by youngsters within the DA, newcomers to the DA and the country at large.

Van Zyl Slabbert – my goodness – I hardly feel qualified to type a sentence summation of that giant's place in our country's history. What a bloody fine liberal. In fact, forget our love affair with Suzman. Frankly, we could have a tough public debate about whether walking out of an apartheid government, as he did, was more morally praiseworthy than was Suzman's decision to remain inside the apartheid state and voice discontent in a limited parliamentary manner.

Both ultimately contributed to the dismantling of apartheid in different ways, of course. My point here is that it is certainly not obvious, despite her name being better known than his, whose role (if we wanted to go there) is actually more morally admirable.

And yet, lo and behold, the DA comes up with a silly video that pretends this man never existed, and when confronted with the omission, lies by pretending that actually we all know about Van Zyl Slabbert anyway.

No we don't! And you, DA strategists, know we don't. If many young black people cannot tell you what Biko did, what makes you think they know who Van Zyl Slabbert was?

Let's be honest here: you think black people will vote for you if you have black struggle heroes and that is the basis on which you decided who to include and exclude.

Suzman could not be left out; she is too big. As is Zille.

The net result is a campaign that assumes black people are history obsessed, and assumes that black people are uncritical and will not see the crude nature of the campaign. But they did, and hence the kinds of angry responses from so many of my radio callers dissing the attempt to pull the wool over their eyes about what happened in history. They did not like the idea of the DA pretending to have had a giant role in history, nor did they want to be enticed to the DA on the basis of history. There's an undeniable dissonance between what I hear on radio and see on social media platforms, and what the DA's amazing, expensive, data-driven, internal scientific research tells it to do.

Ultimately, we will see how effective the campaign was in the 2014 election results. I am not convinced by this confident talk of spreadsheet-politics from the clever strategists. No wonder the ANC always catches up in the weeks leading up to the elections. Common sense is missing here. The black voter is not a data point.

As an aside, it is of course interesting to point out that the DA eventually included more of its leaders in its campaign. But by then the criticism of its initial selectiveness and crude nature had already done damage to the campaign.

Also, the fuller story of the party's history that came later was juxtaposed with other crude moves, like the poster of Nelson Mandela and Helen Suzman side by side. The text accompanying the photo read: 'We played our part in opposing apartheid', and Mandela is seen hugging Suzman in an intimate embrace to create an image that might be more at home in the DA's colour-blind future, it must be said, than our racially segregated past.

It led to a fantastic spoof: a poster of Mandela and Mrs Verwoerd in the same embrace with the same caption.

I mean, really! How many of us have photos of ourselves with Madiba? Imagine if that was all it took to position us as amazing anti-apartheid heroes? Suzman's contribution speaks for itself, but to piggyback on the political and moral symbolism of Mandela with that particular photo is just plain clumsy, frankly. It means that you are desperate to enhance the achievements of Suzman with the additional symbolism of Mandela.

But if that is the aim, you are then moving from telling the story of history to political propaganda. That cheapens the campaign by exposing your earnest claims to merely telling history faithfully. And if it exposes the political motive behind the campaign, then it shows the DA is doing what it always told us only the ANC is capable of, racial politics.

So either way the DA comes out looking horrible here. It is, despite claims to non-racialism, engaging the black voter racially with this appeal to its own black heroes, and by appealing to the endorsement of black icon Mandela, or it is just distorting biographical detail, which is intellectually dishonest in wanting to prop up Suzman's stature by positioning her next to Mandela.

Let's face it. There are many heroes in a revolution. But some heroes are bigger than others. And the DA's communication team again showed a failure to understand the black ANC voter by messing with the black voter's relationship with history and Mandela.

This, by the way, is not the same thing as assuming the black voter is history obsessed. I am not inadvertently conceding the truth behind the DA's basis for this project. Not at all. I am just saying that, among the many mistakes in this campaign is the failure to understand just how much we loved Mandela, and so to score a cheap one by appropriating Mandela in its political campaign is really, again, to treat the black voter as a simpleton.

If the campaign was riddled with all of these errors that underscore the ways in which the DA does not get the black voter then why, you might wonder, does the DA think the campaign was a success?

The reasons are twofold. Firstly, the DA listens to praise singers and blocks out critics. So of course some of the DA supporters really were very happy with this campaign that shows some of its leaders have been involved in the struggle against

apartheid. If you follow DA politicians, or the DA news han-
dles on Twitter, you will know that many people made positive remarks about the campaign that have been retweeted and
cheered by the DA.

But of course like all political parties the DA tends to focus
on the converted, or the newly converted, and not on its critics.
Criticism does not get retweeted.

By simply collating favourable quotes from those who like
the campaign, the party can neatly arrive at the conclusion that
the campaign was a resounding success.

Quite a cool tactic, isn't it?

Except you shoot yourself in the foot, of course, because you
rob yourself of the opportunity of listening to people who are
not just criticising you for the hell of it, but who, if you listened
to them with an open mind, could potentially become new DA
supporters.

The DA cannot afford to listen only to the already- or
nearly-converted.

The second reason behind the DA's gloating is equally interesting. For some reason – quite healthy for our democracy –
the ANC panicked! It responded to the campaign in the most
over-the-top manner. It assumed it a crime against humanity
to compete with its version of history instead of just remaining
calm and confident that its supporters and voters would – as
they did – respond critically to the DA without the help of irate
ANC leaders screaming from the rooftops.

Not only did the ANC release statements and its leaders contest the heinous attempt by the DA to pull the wool over South Africans' eyes about who Mandela belongs to, who liberated South Africans, etc., they went as far as wanting to have a motion tabled in Parliament about it.

Now you can just imagine what music this was to DA strategists' ears. They could not possibly have predicted this over-the-top response from ANC leaders. All they had wanted was for the voters to reconsider them as historically relevant! But here was the ANC radically overreacting, allowing the DA to get even more PR mileage out of the investment than they could have hoped for.

But this reaction from the ANC was not a sign of the campaign's success among potential new DA supporters and voters. The incident only showed that the DA was able to control the news agenda for a couple of weeks because of unexpected paranoia from some ANC leaders.

It is fun to have the ANC want to debate your campaign in Parliament. Fine, I too would sleep with a smile on my face if I was DA communications director Gavin Davis. But the attention it attracted is the wrong measure of success for an election campaign. It is not Gwede Mantashe or the chief whip you are trying to reach. It is Joe Soap in Alexandra.

But because the DA has consistently ignored critics and focused on fans, and because a rattled ANC leadership was perceived as an indication of the campaign's success, you can see why the DA might be really chuffed with itself, but why it shouldn't actually be chuffed with itself. In reality the campaign underscores my main criticism: the DA does not get the complexity of the relationship between an ANC voter and the ANC.

So, what are the implications for the DA if one then accepts that the ANC voter has many motives for her ANC vote, is not irrational, wants services to be delivered, but is also not beyond identity politics like voters the world over *and* has a rich sense of history but is not a slave to history? Specifically, what are the implications of these facts for how the DA should engage the ANC?

RETHINKING DA COMMUNICATIONS: ACCEPTING THE ANC VOTER AS RATIONAL

First, the DA really should not bother spending a massive amount of time and money trying to compete with the ANC's liberation credentials. As Tony Leon rightly pointed out when interviewed about this, the DA should rather sell itself as a party of the future because it will never be able to take on the ANC in debates about the struggle narrative. It is plain silly to go there when black South Africans have such a deep, rich and emotional connection to the past, and one in which black African heroes feature prominently as the main leaders, and as the main sufferers who bore the brunt of the apartheid state's brutal violence.

White liberals just cannot match that. And, sorry, but the black leaders in the DA just cannot match the deeper historical footprints of the ANC's giants. If the DA wants to induce a very macabre public debate about relative contributions to history, even great black leaders like De Lille will fall short next to countless ANC leaders. It just isn't worth going there. Not a low-hanging fruit at all.

Second, the DA has to face an unfortunate truth about race. ANC voters do not just want to see black leaders in the DA before they are prepared to consider the DA a real alternative home to the ANC. In that sense, simply foregrounding the black leaders the party currently has isn't going to work. Black voters can afford to be fussy when it comes to the DA in a way in which the voter is less fussy when it comes to the ANC.

The reason for this is interesting but perfectly coherent. Given their relationship with brand ANC, the ANC supporters protest in their municipality but want services to be delivered by men and women who look like them, who speak like them, who sound like them, and who share their political identity and historical roots.

But the black voter has no such loyalty or historic bond with the DA. None. Obviously. And what this means is that the black voter can look at the DA far more dispassionately and critically than they do the ANC. It is not rocket science at all.

So the desire to see leaders in the DA with whom they can identify should not be simplistically reduced to skin colour. It is about identity, for sure, but not merely about skin colour as such. If we had constituencies, for example, in which we stood for national elections, someone like white DA leader Athol

Trollip would surely have a good chance of winning a constituency seat in the Eastern Cape where he is from, over black DA leader Lindiwe Mazibuko.

The black voter's identity politics need to be engaged more intelligently. Identity is certainly in massive part about race, but it is not only about race. It is also about language, colour, ethnicity, class, geography, and other traits.

The DA would begin to worry the ANC for the first time, in any serious way, if its strategists started asking themselves what it might mean for the next video or next poster campaign to think of black people's identity in these more layered ways.

The challenge, of course, might stump them.

Unfortunately for the DA, the ANC has a head start here. The ANC does not need to have a workshop on how to engage black communities.

Why? Because ANC leaders come from these areas, and more importantly, the thousands of ANC volunteers, branch members and foot soldiers unleashed during the election period actually live these layered identities. It is not academic for them. It is not an intellectual exercise. It just is their very uncomplicated everyday reality. The ANC speaks their language. The ANC is part of their language.

The DA is perhaps more culturally disadvantaged here than many DA leaders have the ability to even truly grasp.

But, at the very least, the DA needs to become conscious of the fact that in engaging the ANC, and the current ANC voter and supporter in attempts to win her over, it needs to be mindful that it is not simply facing racial identity politics, but complex identity politics.

Third, the DA really needs to stop pretending that critics are people who are beyond the pale of political persuasion. I, for example, am probably someone many people within the party would have to, if it is consistent, regard as beyond the pale – a voter who has no intention of ever voting for the DA. Because that is what the DA does when it is confronted with a critic – it dismisses them as inherently uninterested in the party.

Well, let's ask the obvious. Why on earth would I spend so much time writing a book (which is really not a glamorous process despite the joy of book launches and book tours after the fact) if I were not within reach of being persuaded to vote for the party or, who knows, even joining the party at some point?

I have noticed a pattern. When I criticise the ANC as an analyst, or just when I am in comment mode on social media platforms, DA fans endorse my content with glee. When they need to step up to the plate, however, for example when a DA leader or supporter makes a mistake, they are all woefully silent. A case in point was when Helen Zille went out of control, calling some of our internationally respected civil society leaders on public health matters the 'Aids Gestapo' because they showed her up for her evidence-insensitive proposal that we criminalise the transmission of HIV with no regard to what experts had long been saying about the issue in terms of the public health risks of such a policy proposal, however well intentioned.

DA leaders pretended nothing was happening.

The point is that the party comes across to many black voters as consisting of hard-headed, know-it-all, mostly white leaders who think they have a monopoly on the solutions to our problems. How about showing humility when you make mistakes? How about conceding when a critic makes a salient point? Sadly, intransigence is part of all politicians' DNA. For the DA, however, the cost is higher than for an incumbent ruling ANC with over 60% of the vote. And this is why a more actively listening DA, which engages critics and not just fans, would develop a more appealing brand among would-be voters.

Fourth, the DA needs to stop obsessing about data. So here's a conundrum but one that can be solved easily. Yes, throughout this chapter I have, in a sense, been on a mission to show that the DA needs to regard black people as more complex.

But that does not mean that the tools of communication needed to engage with this complexity would also have to be complex. Put simply, if I see you as a human being with a complex psychology, I can still steal your heart with simple techniques – if my techniques are well chosen. So I don't want to be misunderstood. I am not trying to pretend that politics is rocket science in terms of the processes required to maximise the chances of someone voting for you.

I am setting this up carefully so as to present a longstanding gripe I have with DA strategists who obsess about number-crunching, data dumps and spreadsheets. One example of this was when a DA strategist, ahead of the ANC's Mangaung conference, felt very proud of himself for managing to dig up data about just how badly the ANC is actually running Mangaung itself.

The exercise was flaunted on the net, and of course the comment section got plenty of praise from DA fans and ANC haters.

But it is obvious that people in Mangaung do not give a rat's behind for the number-crunching done at 2 am and presented in heavy, boring, thesis-style online articles written by self-indulgent DA researchers. The aim is to destroy the ANC voter's confidence in the ANC and, beyond that, to persuade them to take a chance on your party, the DA. How does spreadsheet politics achieve that?

It doesn't. Rather, live in the spaces where the voters who voted ANC in Mangaung live. Visit them. And not just so as to quickly take a picture for Twitter before heading back to Jozi for lunch in the suburbs. Immerse yourself in their grievances, their desires, their issues. And do not whip out the spreadsheet.

That is not to say that information about a community is irrelevant. Obviously not. But the DA communications team hasn't worked out how to use data as an aid only, and sparingly. Rather, data, and numbers in particular, become something they rely slavishly upon.

I think the reason is simple. They are scared to sit down, look Gogo in the eye, and simply chat. Why? Because it will be jarring. Because we don't live in each other's worlds. So when you speak to someone you don't normally engage with, understand, reach out to, it is – let's face it – bloody awkward and clumsiness lurks just around the corner.

Finally, the DA must focus first on what it will do differently in our communities before it focuses on the ANC's mistakes. To its credit, it does get this point although some of its senior leaders are so accustomed to being in permanent yapping mode that they ignore their own internal research output that has told them that ANC supporters are turned off when the ruling party is attacked aggressively.

As a matter of political strategising, the party needs a tonal shift from yapping to more inclusive, solution-oriented dialogue. Not, ultimately, because the voter doesn't want to hear the ANC being dissed too badly and too often (although that may be true) but because the voter hasn't yet seriously imagined the DA to be a government-in-waiting. And if the party's communications shifted to that kind of focus, then our own attitude towards it might just change accordingly.

* * *

All of these strategic communication changes would help the DA to reposition its brand among voters who currently do not trust the party, who sharply criticise the party and vote for the ANC. But in order to make inroads among these voters, the DA must disabuse itself of the notion that it faces a glass ceiling. It might be true that some blacks, for example, wouldn't ever vote for them, just as some of the men in my community still support the All Blacks and hate the Springboks. But in my view a smaller number of ANC voters are beyond persuasion than the DA realises. Given just how much trouble the ANC brand is in – think corruption, inefficiency and leadership crises that come and go within the alliance; systemically unethical conduct among political principals and civil servants; poor service delivery in many places; the uncontested realities of high unemployment; deep levels of poverty and gross and worsening inequality – I believe an ANC voter could be persuaded to jump ship.

It is the DA that needs to change, not the ANC voter. And the DA needs to change by reimagining what the voter they are engaging is like. And that is: rational; fussy but not recalcitrant; identity-driven but in layered ways not reducible to skin colour; possessing a deep sense of history but not held hostage by imagery from history; not keen on being patronised; suspicious of parties that do not demonstrate an understanding of their world or headspace; and one who cares for service delivery but preferably from a government it identifies with.

If the DA cannot be bothered to meet these challenges, then it can forget about the 30% vote share it aims to get in the 2014 elections. And the ANC would be safe despite its record in government.

BUT … we will know over time whether the DA has the foresight to rethink how it engages the ANC, and the ANC supporter.

7

HAMBA KAHLE, HELEN ZILLE!

How does Helen compare with Tony?

What have Helen's greatest achievements been?

Has Helen now overstayed her welcome?

To be honest, I feel sorry for Helen Zille sometimes. Specifically as leader of the DA she must feel a bit like she's stuck in the Hotel California: you can check out anytime you want, but you can never leave. There is no one who can currently replace her, and so even though she has been willing to step down as party leader, senior leaders would have none of it, including some of those who do not always agree with all of her strategic calls.

Let me start by being blunt about my take on Helen Zille. I think Helen Zille is a good leader. She was the perfect person to build an excellent foundation for the DA in the post-Leon years. In fact, I would go a step further and suggest that she hasn't yet been given adequate recognition within the party and within our political landscape for her role in opposition politics.

But, she'd be the wrong person to lead the party beyond 2014. It goes without saying it is too late for her to be ditched ahead of the 2014 elections. But soon after the 2014 elections the DA must search for a new leader.

Zille is starting to damage her own brand, her own legacy, and most worrying of all, the foundations she built. Not everyone who can erect an amazing building also has the ability to maintain that building or to extend it, redesign it, brand it and re-brand it over time. She has, frankly, now overstayed her welcome in the position of party leader. It would be sensible for the party to honour her contribution, have it archived by a biographer, and then say, 'Hamba Kahle!'

So I want to do two things: explain why I think she has been a good leader who built a great foundation for the party, an achievement that is often unacknowledged; and then why she must go pretty soon after the 2014 elections.

HELEN VS TONY

It's very difficult to compare and contrast Tony Leon and Helen Zille as leaders of the DA. This is because, for me at least, some of Tony Leon's critics exaggerate his weaknesses. And so it's easy to hastily talk about Zille's early strengths by contrasting them with comical, but unfair, recollections of Leon's apparent weaknesses.

Tony is often recalled as yapping away like an irritating neighbourhood dog that doesn't want to stop chasing the heels of passers-by.

He was seen as excessively aggressive in tone, uncritically adopting Westminster-style politics and assuming that this was what we were out to recreate here in the new South Africa, with no cultural sensitivity on how to adapt to black South Africans in Parliament and other South Africans who have very different communication habits to the English. The famous example of this testosterone-loaded politics in overdrive was the 1999 campaign slogan with which Leon's DA spearheaded their election campaign: 'Fight back'. It sounded uncannily like 'Fight black!' of course, and came across as an aggressive attempt to take back the country from the blacks who were running it into the ground.

Both inside and outside the party, this kind of messaging was seen as confirmation that Tony's style of politics had run its course. The party could not be screaming at the ANC and also hope to endear itself to ANC voters who were disappointed with the party they loved but also loved to hate at times.

And, since white nationalists and conservatives were dying out politically, there was little need to placate *them* with that kind of rhetoric, and so the party could afford to – in fact *had* to – start investing in a style of politics that would attract non-traditional supporters.

Tony, with an image of someone straight out of a movie about Prime Minister's Questions (PMQs) in England, could not be the right person.

I used to think that about Leon myself. But, with the wonderful benefit of that thing called 'hindsight', I think this view of

Leon is unfair. Maybe I'm a little biased here, I guess, 'cause I am trained in adversarial competitive debate, and spent a few years at the Oxford Debate Union. When I lived in England I was addicted to episodes of PMQs.

I think England is pretty cool as a model of how to hold the prime minister – or a president – accountable, and the hard-hitting style and quick flow of questioning hurled in the direction of the country's leader on a weekly basis is good for accountability.

In turn, I think the skill of being able to construct arguments quickly, and to deconstruct others' quickly, and to articulate your insights, clearly, logically and with rhetorical flourish, are skills that help to ensure quality public debate on policy questions and social and political issues that matter to a country.

Those were, and still are, skills that Leon had in abundance, and which were on display in Parliament as he role-modelled what it meant to be leader of the opposition in a parliamentary democracy immediately after apartheid's demise in a society that had no such model of its own to draw on.

And in that sense, Leon gets a raw deal around dinner tables and braais, when snide remarks are made about how embarrassingly aggressive he was. Consider a couple of things.

First, as a white South African, he could easily have felt too guilt-ridden to challenge a predominantly black-led government as uncompromisingly as he did. It is a mark of political strength that he respected his own political rights, and citizenship duty in fact, to get on with the job of opposition parliamentary leader and ask the tough questions, in a sustained manner, without being politically crippled by his own racial identity.

Second, I really tire of convincing people how crucial an analytic approach to debate is for a young democracy. Some people labour under the incredibly dangerous assumption that you have to be a hundred years old as a democracy before you can ask really hard questions, sometimes in a tough tone, of those in power.

(This isn't just restricted to party politics, by the way. I used to get the same in the media. I had to work hard to convince media owners at the start of my career a few years ago to give me a radio or TV show on which to air critical debate. The fear was that the public could only handle platforms where we had our say, listened to each other, 'heard each other', and then went our separate ways, chuckling with rainbow-nation flags draped around us … What rubbish! I am glad the public has proven these fears wrong with their huge appetite for critical dialogue.)

The same applies to parliamentary debate. It is young democracies, *more so* than so-called mature democracies, that need processes that facilitate accountability to be entrenched quickly and deeply; precisely so that a culture of accountability is entrenched as soon as possible.

And one of the most fundamental elements of liberal democracy that requires entrenchment early on in the life of a new democracy is what the ANC labels, but doesn't always practise, *robust debate*.

The Tony Leon we often lampoon, ironically enough, is the

Tony Leon that is a good poster person for robust debate, which is worth promoting in a young democracy.

It's funny, isn't it, that we can expect ourselves to be ready for these kinds of practices in twenty or thirty years' time but we are too scared to practise the future that we want to arrive at. How odd.

So, not only in the first instance was Leon correct to set aside racial self-consciousness and get on with asking tough questions of our first black-led democratic government, he was also, on a more philosophical level, role-modelling a crucial aspect of liberal democratic politics: accountability and the key tool with which to achieve it: robust debate.

Now, before critics of Tony get excited, I definitely am not implying he was a perfect political leader or suggesting perhaps he should re-enter the party now (though some might want to debate that idea, actually). Tony and I disagree profoundly on what liberalism means, on whether or not race-based policies are morally justifiable, quite apart from whether or not they can work, etc.

And I think that many of his ideas, even now, are too right-wing to serve a country that is still battling the scars of deep social injustices off the back of apartheid.

So I would not vote for him to be the party's next leader (again) after Helen's exit.

It is crucial to recall that I wrote earlier in this book that the DA's engagement with the public and the ANC is often tone deaf. I think many would be astounded if I thought Leon's communication style was beyond reproach and that only the current crop of DA leaders made tonal mistakes. That is not what I am implying here. Tony had communication weaknesses too.

Tony lacked stylistic *range*. A politician needs to be able to communicate in different styles, on different occasions, in different settings, depending on what is called for in that context. Like most DA leaders now, for the most part Leon did not have stylistic range in his armoury as a communicator. That was a communication weakness that didn't help perceptions that he was an aggressive white man annoyed with black power.

Leon could deliver a hard-hitting speech in Parliament and debate brilliantly in an interview or in a town hall, but the softer speech that demonstrates empathy with the person being engaged wasn't something Tony knew much about, like others in the DA.

In that respect, he was a one-trick pony. But I really think that the trick that the pony performed should not be dissed. It is a trick that is crucial in a healthy democracy. The more appropriate criticism is to lament an absence of *other ways of speaking*.

My point here, then, is that many sketches of Tony's style of politics, and his approach to parliamentary politics in particular, remain grossly unfair.

I admire his capacity for reasoned debate and think he had a great grasp of the oversight role of an opposition party.

Nevertheless, perceptions are crucial in politics. And so the party that Helen took over was perceived to be one that was lily-white, aggressive in style and character, and punting market-based solutions to the country's problems with no concern for social justice. And the approach of the party's leader was seen by many to epitomise the entitlement of the haves.

Helen's challenge was cut out for her. She had to deal those perceptions a death blow and build, in a very real and systematic way, a party culture and organisation that would appeal to new members and supporters who did not previously find the DA appealing.

She also had to signal something of a break with Leon's legacy, stylistically, but without alienating the core support base of the party.

And this is where Helen deserves massive credit.

If my characterisation of Tony is correct, then Helen's challenge was even bigger than one imagined. On one hand, she had to distance herself from the *perception* that he was an aggressive yapper and promise, and demonstrate, that she would not be that.

And yet, at the same time, deep down, she had to know that he had role-modelled attributes that were, *objectively*, great ones to emulate if we wanted to entrench opposition politics in the new South Africa.

So, in an almost confusing way, she had to be seen to distance herself from his style. Yet at the same time, a certain continuity with his technique and style was, surely, what our democracy required? If she had completely abandoned his relentless commitment to hold the government responsible with strong evidence-based questions and logical, well-constructed argument, delivered with rhetorical flourish, then Parliament and opposition politics more generally would be weaker.

So, what to do?

I think, years later, it is clear that Helen managed to achieve exactly that balance. One of her key strengths is precisely the same kind of relentless, inquisitorial approach to the opposition leadership role that Tony had adopted. The key difference is that under her leadership the party split the role of party leader so that the leader in Parliament was not the same as the leader outside Parliament. This too was an achievement.

Firstly, by splitting this role, Helen dealt with the 'yapping' perception problem. Here the party, and not just Zille, deserves credit. By sharing Leon's problematic image between a leader outside Parliament, and a leader inside Parliament, it instantly became impossible for any one person in the DA to ever again be the singular focus of media reporting or ANC attention.

This is not a permanent party position now, but in a sense Leon had become too prominent as the face and voice of the party. This is not to deny the incredible influence of many other senior DA leaders throughout this time including, obviously, Sandra Botha who then led the DA inside Parliament, or others like Douglas Gibson whose effectiveness had to be neutered with diplomatic offerings abroad.

But by not being inside Parliament, where Leon's perception as a yapper had been cemented, Helen managed to effect a shift. This was a shrewd move. So much so that many, myself included, often talk about a stylistic break from Leon's approach to opposition politics. But I think talk of a stylistic break is actually nonsense. It is just a reflection of how much we are and were fooled by the fact that Helen is not in Parliament, and Tony was.

If you listen to how Helen speaks, her tone, her engagement with the media, with ANC politicians, and now increasingly with those she disagrees with on social media platforms and among civil society activists and organisations, it is blatantly obvious that she is just as muscular and hard-headed as Leon ever was. There is more continuity than discontinuity in style between them. I will discuss a few examples shortly in motivating why she should go soon after the 2014 elections.

The problem, as with Tony, is that if you do not mix up your styles of engagement, and you become a one-trick pony, you have limited impact in how you come across as a leader. And of course that's what has happened now.

But on the constructive side, Zille's willingness to be relentless in holding the ANC government accountable, and her capacity to be hard on a public that doesn't vote for her party in provinces where the ANC governs but then asks her what the DA can do for them (to which she often sarcastically responds on Twitter along the lines of, 'Vote for me and we can show you'), also demonstrate an ability to get on with the democratic burden and privilege of being the leader of the official opposition (outside Parliament). She too is not crippled by her skin colour, and takes the fight to the ANC.

We really cannot afford to have white South Africans retreating into the suburbs, being coy about their citizenship, or opting out of political leadership or politics generally. White South Africans are, to state the obvious, citizens and as such have an entitlement – a duty even – to actively participate in public, political processes. And Zille role-models, just as Leon did, how to have a sense of ownership about this weird and wonderful country of ours despite our divisive past, and despite the incredible brand power of the incumbent governing party, the ANC.

I would imagine, then, that if I was a member or supporter of the DA, she might be someone who would be quite easy to admire, and to be inspired by, even: hardworking and fearless, demonstrably committed to the democratic project, with a firm grasp of the role of the opposition in a liberal democratic society borne out daily in her leadership.

But Zille's greatest achievement, I think, is to have managed to make the DA a place sexy enough for many young people, black and white, to start flocking to. Sure, its youth wing cannot compete in numbers yet with the Young Communist League or the ANC Youth League. But that sort of comparison would miss the point of what is happening in our political landscape.

Across South African university campuses, student politics

in the 1990s used to be dominated by knock-off organisations inspired by black political parties and organisations. Middle-class kids of all colours either didn't take part or, if they did, joined one of these party wings, or ran for leadership positions on the campuses as independent candidates.

And then, just as Zille managed the perceptions of the post-Leon years, she also managed to sell the story of a DA that was more *inclusive*, a story about building a South Africa in which everyone had opportunities to be the best individual they could be.

The inclusivity message started to resonate with many, but even more importantly, rather than just talking the talk, provincial party structures started *acting* more systematically to set up branches in communities and on campuses. This is why, for example, Makashule's story that I told earlier is possible. The party became a well-oiled machine that knew it needed to set it-self up as a party that had a wider presence. This organisational change had to go hand in hand with a change in organisational culture and messaging.

And it is these changes in the immediate post-Leon years that enabled Helen's DA to grow as well as it then did. This is why, today for example, I can sit in Rosebank with a DA politician and listen for hours to him talking to me in great detail about the complex DA branch politics in a township like Alexandra, branch politics that now have a long history already. Because the DA has been present for a while already, despite being lampooned by ANC politicians.

It is also for this reason that the DA under Helen has increased its support among black African voters who are older. So it is not just coconut youngsters who are joining. Of course, we are still talking about small numbers in percentile terms, and these numbers are disputed between the party's number-crunchers and some analysts like Ebrahim Fakir who is an elections specialist.

But the true magnitude of the DA's share of the black vote now, and the dispute about it, should not detract from the praise due to Zille. Under her leadership, brand DA has become much more appealing to young people – black and white – than before, and certainly there is an upward trajectory in the numbers of black people – young and old – who are joining the DA or supporting it. Zille's hard work is responsible for these changes. The party is indebted to her leadership.

Last, though controversial, I think Helen also deserves credit for some perceptive (though not perfect) mentorship. Mmusi Maimane's career would not be where it is without her heavy hand. She secretly bullies many people into ensuring certain kinds of voting outcomes in leadership contests. And some young leaders, like Mmusi, benefit from her support. The same goes for Lindiwe Mazibuko.

If Helen, for example, had supported Athol Trollip rather than Lindiwe Mazibuko for the position of parliamentary leader, Lindiwe would be nowhere today. Or she would still be a prominent national spokesperson and Mmusi would be far less prominent.

So Helen has the ability to own a tactical decision she has thought long and hard about, and whether you agree with her or not, she then runs with it and asks the party to trust her, and to judge her on the basis of whether or not her instincts yield returns for the party in terms of new voters and new supporters. Clearly, so far, the numbers are on her side.

This ability to take tough decisions, like nurturing young black talent in a party with a traditional strong white support base, is leadership excellence. I am honestly not sure if Lindiwe Mazibuko or Mmusi Maimane would have emerged inside the DA under Leon's watch.

I just don't think Tony had Zille's pragmatism. That is one profound difference between them, and on some level it also represents a clear ideological break. Sure, both of them want to live in a colour-blind South Africa where we see 'content of character' and not skin colour. And Helen would publicly pretend, of course, that her preference for Lindiwe and Mmusi has only to do with their talents. She would pretend to share Leon's definition of non-racialism: a society in which race is not salient.

But Helen is profoundly aware that race, in reality, matters. And in fact she is a pragmatist in a way that has enormously transformed the DA in the wake of Tony's exit. If it wasn't for her pragmatism, Mmusi, Lindiwe, Makashule and even Wilmot James would not be part of the top leadership structure of the DA.

Many senior leaders in the party hate her guts. Some of them do not even respect Mmusi. But they cannot push back because

Helen's tactics are vindicated where it matters – in an upward trajectory at the polls.

So, since Helen has had to pretend – in line with her party's chosen philosophy of colour-blindness – that she doesn't believe in race-based affirmative action, let me then, as writer, do the honours and affirm her pragmatic brilliance in punting young black talent.

It has been a fine strategy beyond the Tony years. And the party would not have followed this path but for Helen's insistence. It is one of her greatest achievements, and the right thing to have done.

Finally, she needs credit for even being willing to step down. Sadly we live in a political culture where people overstay their welcome. Few people outside the party are aware that Helen is not hellbent on staying on as leader, even as I type this sentence. She has previously told the leadership of the party just that. But they panicked at the prospect of her letting go of the position, because they do not know who would replace her.

I think people might be surprised to know that she has been willing to step down. But this surprise would be a reflection of how we confuse someone's energetic defence of positions in policy and other debates with their unwillingness to step down from leadership positions.

Helen might be hard-headed about her convictions, but she is perfectly capable of reflecting on the limitations of her being in the role of party leader. That, too, is a leadership strength that needs acknowledgement.

BUT HERE'S THE SNAG …

All of these leadership strengths and contributions, acknowledged and unacknowledged, are a matter of history. Or will be once it is all properly archived. This chapter is really a plea that Helen be given some historical justice when we look back at her career.

But, as I said, Helen is not the right person to lead the party beyond the 2014 elections. Ideally, in fact, the DA should have gone into the 2014 elections with someone else at the helm.

The DA won't, in our lifetime, become the party in government in South Africa if it isn't led by a black South African. It probably has to be led by a black African in particular. But the DA can most definitely kiss outright electoral victory in our lifetime goodbye if it continues to be led by a white South African.

Now, let's not pretend that this is theoretical nonsense. You have to live in cloud cuckoo land to think that race doesn't matter in South Africa. We can make a case that race *shouldn't* matter. (I think it does, but there's a debate here to be had elsewhere.) But it does matter, and that is the starting point from which most political strategising happens. Unless, of course, winning elections is not the reason you are in politics. Which would be bizarre.

I'm not interested here in whether this is a tragic fact about our country, or whether we should challenge the electorate to think differently. The reality is that unless the DA is led by a black African, the party will not unseat the ANC.

Obviously, being led by a black African will not be enough. Many other issues, addressed throughout this book, would have to fall into place. And, of course, not just any black African leader will do. In logical language, one might say that a black African leader is a necessary but not a sufficient condition for the DA to be able to beat the ANC in a general election in the next few general elections. Such is the reality of race in our country. And that is reason enough for Helen to go.

She knows this well, of course. Which is why she is perfectly comfortable with (though mistaken about) the idea of Mamphela Ramphele taking over from her (more on this in chapter 8). Helen knows that she will not be president of South Africa. If it was up to her, she would simply be the Premier of the Western Cape, and Mamphela, or someone like her, would lead the party and challenge the dominance of the ANC among black African voters.

Helen is not black enough and we are not colour-blind enough as voters.

I have no doubt that many DA hacks will fume at what I just wrote, and even quote the previous sentence as a perfect example of a writer thinking for others. I do not fear such defensiveness from party hacks. For one thing, it is the DA, and not writers about politics, who want to get into power, so they would do well to be less hard-headed about critical dialogue.

Much more important than this response, however, is the fact that the DA itself is in agreement with me. There is no way in hell that Mmusi Maimane would have been picked as the DA's

Gauteng Premier candidate over the experienced Jack Bloom if Mmusi wasn't black. It is an open secret that Mmusi's race was a deal-breaker in his favour.

I challenge any DA leader to look me in the eye and say, 'Eusebius, if Jack Bloom was black, Mmusi would still have been elected the Premier candidate for Gauteng.' I'm afraid I'd then have to resort to my native Afrikaans, '*Jy's 'n liegbek!*' ('You're a liar!')

(The only trait that Mmusi has in greater abundance than Jack, and which is relevant to his candidacy, is charisma, but the wealth of technical knowledge and governance experience on Jack's part just makes him too strong for the charisma gap to be enough for Mmusi to be the correct candidate, especially since Jack isn't a monster, but actually known across Gauteng ... But, all of this means nothing, of course, in the face of Mmusi's beautiful black skin.)

And so, as with their pragmatic choice of black Mmusi as Premier candidate for Gauteng, so too in the name of pragmatism must they ditch Helen for a black leader soon after 2014.

But there is a second reason Zille has overstayed her welcome. It has nothing to do with her race, I'm afraid. In the last two years especially, she has simply become unable to recognise when she is making disastrous leadership calls. And because she has achieved a lot as party leader, many of her peers, although otherwise confident, do not call her out on blunders that cost her, and cost the party.

When a leader has reached this kind of cult status in an organisation then it is best for them to leave. It is good to have a
leader who can take decisions without being scared to do so,
like her nurturing of young black talent. But the other extreme
is a charismatic leader whose mistakes go unchecked because
there is a limit to how much people around her are willing to
push back given that she is larger than life inside the party.

The one clear example, raised in an earlier chapter in a different
context, is Helen's disastrous intervention in the policy debate on
HIV/Aids, specifically about whether or not to criminalise the
transmission of HIV. The usual DA loudmouths who are quick to
point out political idiocy among ANC leaders simply froze when
Helen referred to some of our country's most well-respected, internationally renowned Aids activists as 'Aids Gestapo'.

It was a complete strategic and communications disaster. The
language, the tone, and even the content of her viewpoint were
way off the mark. I interviewed her on Talk Radio 702 about it
and it was clear she wasn't even familiar with the literature on
whether or not it was a good public health policy proposal to
chuck people in jail for transmitting HIV.

So far off the mark was Helen that even Helen Epstein, on
whose research she relied (singularly and uncritically one must
add too), had to write an article saying that the other Helen was
drawing the wrong conclusions from her work.

But here's the point. Helen was arrogant, pretending to be
an expert, refusing to climb down after hurling abuse at civil
society experts, and unable, most importantly of all, to see that

as opposition leader you need civil society on your side as you fight the ANC, and as you persuade the electorate to vote for you.

She just could not find it in herself to show humility, and it took forever and a day before her penchant for Twitter wars started to subside. Way too long. And where were the strong DA leaders who are so quick to go after ANC politicians when they behave stupidly on policy positions about which they know nothing?

Silent. And why? Because of the cult status around Helen. This is another reason she must go. Yes, you want a leader who is fearless. But you also want a leader who does not lack the ability to reign themselves in, the ability to sense vulnerability, and to know when their actions and utterances are beginning to damage the brand of the party.

I do not think Helen has these instincts now in the same supply as she had them before. She has become too successful for her own good. And that is hurting the party, and her own legacy.

WHAT DOES THIS MEAN FOR ME, THE VOTER?

When I see Helen continuing to be irritated with civil society (even now), I think to myself, 'My God, she is no better than the ANC! She hates criticism as much as the ANC! THAT's why Simphiwe Dana annoys her! THAT's why she cannot stand Equal Education! And that's why, most bizarre of all, she is even willing to defend Angie Motshekga against Equal Education!'

Is mine the kind of reaction you want from a voter? Perceiving your party leader in the Western Cape as behaving uncannily like the leaders of the ANC elsewhere? No, of course not. Because then the incentive to vote for the DA is destroyed.

If I think the ANC is horrible towards civil society movements and their leaders, why on earth would I take a chance on a party led by someone who thinks that Zackie Achmat is the Aids Gestapo? Let's face it, that sounds like Thabo Mbeki, and we know what we think of his legacy on tolerating rational approaches to policy debate and tolerating civil society.

So an out-of-control Helen Zille, even if she were pitch black and could not speak English to save her life, would still be a liability for the DA beyond 2014.

But she is white. And, yes, race still matters, and will for years still to come. In that context, even if her advisers could fix her communication glitches, she must still step down because the party needs to be led by a black leader if it is to make a serious attempt at challenging the ANC.

Who should replace her? I haven't a clue! But that doesn't change the problem that her staying on represents. She had a great innings, but it's time to retire as party leader.

8

TO MERGE OR
NOT TO MERGE?

Should the **DA** ever have offered their top leadership
post to Mamphela Ramphele?

Under what conditions should the **DA** accept
politicians from other parties?

Is there intrinsic value to political diversity?

doubt my hesitation about voting DA is going to be settled by debates about mergers within the opposition ranks. But the DA thinks a merger debate is relevant to me as a potential DA voter, which is why there has been a lot of internal debate about whether or not to parachute in leaders from other parties and, if so, who they should be. There has also been a lot of debate about whether or not the DA should merge or cooperate in some other way with the smaller opposition parties.

Several things go through my mind when I see these political games going on. I see a desperation to make the DA attractive to me by finding help from outside the party. It's almost like an implicit concession that the existing leadership, and the existing set of ideas within the party, won't do the trick of luring me into the party.

Ideally, I'd have liked a party to be able to say, 'Hey, Eusebius, the people and ideas we currently have PERFECTLY match your needs! Come on in ...' But by fishing around in the wider opposition pool for help, I kinda think this is a party that accepts it is deeply flawed, and unable to match the desires of voters who don't currently find it attractive.

That said, though, it isn't a huge turn-off seeing the DA worry about the state of the entire opposition, and engaging in debates about possible cooperation with other parties. On a positive note, it makes me think that I am unfair to write off the party as extremely hard-headed at times. Because if it is asking itself whether or not to merge with smaller parties, it is at least, for once, thinking about me the voter who has problems with the existing apparatus, and not just going full-steam ahead in imposing that apparatus on me, in a sort of 'take it or leave it!' fashion.

And so, in that vein, I think it is worth rewarding the DA by puzzling through the merger question with them. I don't think merging will help entice me to the party, and the aim of this chapter is, simply, to set out the case for my view.

MY OVERALL TAKE ...

I can see no good reason why the DA should go out of its way to gobble up smaller opposition parties. The DA has less to gain, and a bit to lose, by merging with smaller parties. These smaller parties in turn have a lot more to gain – like not imploding – and very little, if anything, to lose by merging with the DA.

The real issue is whether or not the DA should merge with

Agang SA and, in that scenario, whether Mamphela Ramphele should become the leader of a new political party that results from such a merger.

This is a bad idea for the DA. Or so I think.

I wanna explain why the DA leaders who were secretly fuming when Zille was holding talks to persuade Mamphela to join the DA were right to be fuming. Fortunately for these leaders, of course, Mamphela was silly enough to ignore the offer of a free political party – for no guarantee of bringing in hundreds of thousands of voters – and decided to form her own party. It was, in retrospect, a blessing in disguise for the DA that Mamphela made the mistake of not accepting this gift-horse.

But Zille still has a yearning for possibly bringing Mamphela into the DA. So the merger conversation is a live option, and it is worth discussion here because the folly of such a proposal helps to shed light – again – on just how out of touch the DA is at times with what it needs to do to be more appealing to black African voters.

But let's systematically examine the arguments for a merger.

THE MULTIPARTY DEMOCRACY ARGUMENT

One half-baked justification for a merger that people sometimes throw about is the fact that smaller parties are dwindling. If you look at the black consciousness-based parties, or even a bigger party like the IFP (the most dramatic example maybe), their share of the vote has steadily declined with each successive election. And they are facing extinction. A new entrant like Cope did all right, capturing some 1.4 million votes and just above 7% in the last general elections, but it doesn't require a political scientist to figure out that smaller parties are dying out, and the romance of multiparty democracy is being killed like a fart spoiling a good date.

I think, even though people don't always say so, support for a consolidated opposition is often secretly based on an obsession with keeping as many political parties, and politicians, politically alive as possible.

Related to this, obviously, is the desire to make sure that as many political ideas and ideologies remain within our body politic.

This would not be a compelling argument for the DA to enter into merger talks with smaller parties.

The problem here is an obsession with diversity for its own sake. If you have gone out of political fashion, then tough luck. If no one wants the African Christian Democratic Party (ACDP), or the UDM, or Cope, then why should the DA throw them a lifeline in the name of multiparty democracy? I've never understood what the *intrinsic* value of political diversity is.

Think of it this way. Do we think it is a tragedy that Lion Lager is no longer sold everywhere? Yeah, my dad gets all nostalgic and stuff about the Lions he downed during the 1980s, and we all remember the brand when we think of the Lion Cup in rugby (including a tog bag my dad had with the logo on it), but products come and go.

Take a more recent example: BlackBerry is pretty soon going to be as toast as Nokia. It is already embarrassing to take out your BlackBerry and put it on the table. Products, as I said, come and go.

Politicians, too, come and go. Ideas come and go. Political parties come and go. And the point of democracy is that it is, at its core, a popularity contest. If the ACDP cannot sell Christianity to the nation as a basis for a political programme, then it should pack up and try opening churches perhaps.

So my advice, in turn, to those who are romantic about multiparty democracy is to reflect on why they have an obsession with *diversity for its own sake*. If NO ONE ever takes the ginger cookie in the box of assorted cookies, should we continue baking that flavour just because a diverse range looks cute?

And I use these analogies seriously, by the way, because I suspect the obsession with diverse political parties and ideologies just is a reflection of an aesthetic pleasure in seeing a Parliament with diverse ideas. (But ask yourself: how much brilliance comes from the colourful, diverse outfits and styles we see at the opening of Parliament?)

I think we should see democracy as a marketplace where people compete to sell their ideas and their parties – and if the ANC and the DA become the two main contenders (just as there are two main contenders in the States), then the market has spoken.

The DA has no democratic duty to rescue ailing smaller parties, nor political ideas that no longer turn voters on.

WILL MERGING WITH SMALL PARTIES MAKE THE DA MORE APPEALING TO NEW VOTERS?

There are some who argue that it might be in the interests of
the DA to consider merging with small parties. For one thing, it
automatically means increasing the number of supporters and
voters of the party, even if only by a few percentage points.

More optimistically, the hope is that if I do not vote for the DA
now, nor for the smaller parties, that I might find a consolidated
opposition party more attractive than the DA as such, and will
be prepared to abandon the ANC ship (assuming I even vote
ANC).

Obviously, there is a massive assumption here about what
drives my reluctance to already be a committed DA supporter
and voter – and, without even yet putting on my hat as an analyst, I think it's obvious that this assumption is not going to hold.

It is highly speculative to assume that what stands between
me and a DA T-shirt is that Mosiuoa or Bantu aren't yet inside
the DA. After all, as a voter I never found these men compelling. So the merger talks, linked to me as a hesitant voter,
seem desperate in their attempts to attract me to the DA. More
worrying for the DA, it means the party is again not getting
why my blood isn't blue yet.

Yet some still insist on imagining that a DA that has in its ranks the likes of Bantu Holomisa, Mosioua Lekota and Mamphela Ramphele suddenly becomes a much stronger proposition than one that contains a mostly senior white leadership with a couple of young black politicians, and stronger than a small party with one senior black struggle hero driving it.

But this is not compelling. For one thing, egos are huge in politics. There would be a massive clashing of heads if all of these leaders were suddenly in one political party. Cope has still not had an elective conference since its founding, for example, because it remains hamstrung by intractable personality squabbles. (At the time of finalising this chapter, in October 2013, Cope's leadership fight had finally come to a legal end, with Lekota declared the leader of the party – but still no elective conference had been held, though one was being promised to party members for December 2013. Even if it were to happen, the party's democratic credentials are in shreds.)

Politicians are by nature ambitious characters – many of them megalomaniacs even – and if you bring them all into one space as a bunch of former party leaders, then you are bound to have complicated negotiations about leadership posts, squabbles about who speaks on what and when, etc. It is a recipe for disaster.

It will also rightly upset many DA leaders and supporters, young and old, black and white, who, over the years, put up with Zille's strong-arm tactics when she helped fast-track the careers of some. But in the event of a merger there will be pushback, and an insistence that the meritocracy that the party preaches be respected by any newcomer who joins.

But while Nosimo Balindlela, the ANC's former Eastern Cape Premier, seems content to work her way through the DA ranks in a bottom-up manner, there is no way in hell a giant like Lekota would be a foot soldier when previously he was an army general in another outfit.

The calculation then is whether the negotiations and tensions that will come with merger talks are worth the potential gains? And the answer, it seems to me, is 'No'. Given that these small parties are disappearing faster than you can say 'save multi-party democracy!' the potential voters they bring to the party do not make the predictable costs of merging worth incurring.

The unknown factor is whether a disgruntled ANC voter who thinks the DA is too white will suddenly join the DA if Holomisa or Lekota are in the party. But I just cannot see why that makes sense. If these voters do not currently rush to join the UDM or Cope – and in fact are running away from these parties – why would one big fat merger magically transform the assessment of these individual politicians in the eyes of voters who have steadily been abandoning these parties?

In addition to these realities, the DA of course also has to worry about its core identity. Now here there is some fluidity. For starters, as I have argued earlier, elections do not fundamentally turn on political ideology or identity in South Africa. So the DA could, if it wanted to, be pragmatic in choosing alliances. There's no need to be precious about 'political ideology' when the first goal in politics is simply to get into political office.

However, the DA has *chosen* to sell itself to the South African public as not being interested in inviting into its ranks any party or politician that does not share its foundational values and principles. But the reality is that mergers cannot just be based on thin agreements such as 'we value democracy, openness, accountability…'

More substantive issues, such as whether or not to adopt race-based policies in response to past injustices, unfettered market-based solutions to key economic challenges, etc., will have to be negotiated. And the party, of course, has the advantage of being able to play hard to get. It can insist that its principles be the ones that must be accepted.

But, it is destined for identity in-fighting. This is not inherently unhealthy, but the ANC will love it when a divided, broad church DA is unable to sing from the same hymn sheet. This tendency has already been apparent in the disagreement between party chairperson Wilmot James, who is opposed to Black Economic Empowerment because he does not believe in policies that use the language of race, and party spokesperson Mmusi Maimane, who is adamant that no longer will the DA be seen as a party that doesn't recognise the need for explicit race-based redress.

This kind of disagreement will be compounded if the DA joins up with smaller parties that have political leaders with deep political ideological convictions that are very different to those of most senior DA leaders. It will be messy and leave the opposition divided rather than organised, united and focused on taking on the ANC behemoth.

So, given how low the chances are of great returns on a merger deal, and how much more certain personality, ideological and policy fights are, it is best that the DA simply ignores the smaller parties and continues to concentrate on being the best DA it can be.

In the event, of course, that a small party dissolves, the DA shouldn't stop that party's members or leaders from joining the DA. But don't treat them as special; let them join as ordinary members, and keep the DA's identity and party processes intact, and fight the ANC machinery with a clear, consistent party identity, rather than as a hodgepodge of opposition parties slapped together with only anti-ANC sentiment as the glue that holds them tentatively together. We saw with Cope what happens when the main basis of an alliance is anti-ANC sentiment: it is a ticking time bomb waiting to explode.

The best model for how to handle a small party that wants to enter the DA is the way the DA handled the Independent Democrats (ID). It threw Patricia a lifeline, but the ID was a walking political corpse, and the DA did not compromise its identity and signature political ideas in the process. It is Patricia, surely, who will be remembered by historians as the great political chameleon.

But I suspect that it would be harder to get the likes of grumpy

Mosioua to acquiesce to the same extent. And that is why the predictable costs of merging aren't worth it when the party has other aspects of its machinery it can work to grow beyond its existing voter base.

WHAT ABOUT DR RAMPHELE?!

'PHEW!' is the favourite response, with a smile, from DA politicians and supporters when I chat to them about Dr Ramphele having abandoned the DA plan to parachute her into the party. At the very last minute she decided to go it alone. The sigh of relief from many was because they did not support an idea that Zille was adamant about.

I think it was a poorly-thought-through idea and the DA should thank the political gods that Ramphele was arrogant and imprudent enough to look a gift-horse in the mouth.

First, from Mamphela's perspective, it should have been a no-brainer. Of course she should have joined the DA! Here you have a party that basically offers itself up to you – with all its infrastructure, its legitimacy, its traction with the voters – and donates to you the role of CEO of the business basically. And for what? For MAHALA! And then what does the good doctor do? She walks away!

It will go down as one of the dumbest political 'No thank yous!' in democratic South Africa, and I do not have the biblical gift of interpretation to explain *why* she did it. Some say that her reported advisers, one Moeletsi Mbeki and one Prince Mashele, had whispered into her ear that she could do well enough on her own at the polls, and only thereafter should she negotiate with the DA and make even more demands than that of being party leader when she merges with the party, for example, insist on senior-level appointments from outside, enforce certain policy changes, and so forth.

If this speculation is correct, I'm afraid it is so high risk that when put next to the guaranteed instant gain of an entire official opposition party, I see no rationality in turning down Zille's offer. However she was thinking about the offer, Mamphela certainly wasn't thinking *like a politician*.

The other possibility is that Mamphela didn't want her political biography messed up by joining party politics in the new South Africa directly via the DA. Perhaps she wanted to soften suggestions of her being a sell-out of history. She could thus keep her political credentials intact by first starting her own party, and then merging with the DA later. This delayed merger might be better received by some segments of the public (at least the segments that might not like someone perceived as a sell-out for not joining the ANC first), than being seen to simply cosy up to the DA as your first attempt to be a party politician.

But this is unlikely. I know as fact that negotiations with the DA were intimate and lengthy, and the deal was scuppered literally at the last minute, so it is more likely that Mamphela was swayed by advice that she go it alone. I think she also banked on the possibility of former senior black leaders from the ANC, Cope, and people in big business joining her outfit, and boosting her new party, thereby upsetting the DA. (But these hopes were subsequently dashed when they didn't join her – think of the likes of the brothers Pityana, Moeletsi Mbeki, Jay Naidoo, and many others – and she now looks like a one-woman band. This is all the more reason why it was such high risk to turn down a political party offered on a silver platter.)

But while Mamphela made a mistake, what about the DA's decision to *offer* her a leadership role? Now this is fascinating. It connects directly with the core issue this books grapples with. The desperation to offer Mamphela the position of leader – which, surprisingly, is still not entirely off the table – again reflects how poorly many DA leaders understand black voters.

The DA, firstly, has again been caught with its non-racialism pants on fire. For a party that insists racial 'bean-counting' is an ANC pastime, why on earth has it been courting Mamphela, an outsider, rather than simply holding internal leadership elections? The answer is obvious: they know that they need a black African leader, and preferably one that is senior, both in age, and in terms of political gravitas.

So the first observation about the courting of Mamphela is that it smashes the DA denial that it cares about race in the same sort of racially realistic way as ANC politicians or the rest of us do. The DA clearly does too. Why else all those negotiations right up to the weekend before Mamphela announced her 'platform' Agang SA at Constitution Hill in Braamfontein? We know that Zille can see black and white too, and the entire DA can too. Don't believe the colour-blind messaging.

But, that's not a bad thing, of course. It is sensible to engage the electorate, as I have insisted, in terms of where the electorate is at, and not only where you want the electorate to be.

But being black is not enough, though. The DA has given no thought to what other qualities in a senior leader are required to gain traction with the electorate. This is the sense in which the obsession with Mamphela, at least on Zille's part, shows a poor understanding of black voters. Although black voters are likely to be more attracted to a DA that looks like the country we all live in, it isn't a case of, 'Any black leader will do.' To repeat: black isn't sufficient; it is just necessary. That is an important mantra to hang on to as these leadership conundrums are worked through within the DA.

So, for example, Helen has many qualities as a political leader that make her, even as a white politician, easier to market than Mamphela. Helen speaks with more energy and is more articulate; she has an easier rapport with ordinary voters; she can jive with some authenticity now, even if still a little clumsily. If I was her campaign manager or chief communications strategist, I'd be more than happy with what I have to work with.

Ramphele, on the other hand, is stilted. She isn't easy on the ear, and will not be memorable when put in a big town hall next to, say, Lindiwe, Buti, Moisuoa, Patricia and even old Mangosuthu. She just doesn't have political charisma. Having a high IQ, or great academic record, or even a good record as a political and social commentator and community activist aren't enough.

Politics is about speeches, connecting with people, being in front of the camera, walking easily in communities, speaking in sound bites. And here, I'm afraid, Mamphela is more like the DA's Wilmot James – best kept in the back room to be consulted behind the scenes.

Honestly, in a constituency-based system, I reckon even in our race-obsessed country, there are some predominantly black constituencies that would vote Helen over Mamphela. Because while race matters, and deeply so, it is not the only thing that matters.

The good news here is that Zille gives herself and the electorate too little credit at times. (For example, as I said, Trollip would trounce Mazibuko in many constituency elections in the Eastern Cape.) The bad news is that the DA also treats black voters as simpletons, and it is this that costs the DA votes because blacks can sniff a party or politician that treats them as such. 'Ah, racial identity and old people matter to them! PHONE RAMPHELE, QUICK!'

And Mamphela, by the way, isn't the only one I could pick on here. Wilmot James, as I intimated, also struggles to be an effective politician. He is essentially a researcher–academic who has entered a political party, landed a top leadership post, and is pretty much parking off there now, with little real political influence and even less public impact.

One of the most recent examples of him not being as influential as he ought to be for a federal chair was when Nosimo Balindlela jumped ship to the DA. The day before Helen made the announcement, I was having dinner with a senior political journalist. We decided to get reaction from Wilmot, since she had a good relationship with him. She called him, and to our surprise, he knew absolutely nothing about it.

And he wasn't bluffing. He confessed that he'd have to make some calls, and find out what was going on but made it clear to my friend that it was the first he had heard of it. Clearly, you can be the federal chair, but live outside the kitchen cabinet of the party's actual leader.

As for Wilmot's impact on the ground, I suspect most people reading this book do not know him, but do know Mmusi, Lindiwe, Athol, Helen, Patricia, etc. That says a lot about how small his public impact is. And it would not be true that even on his own turf, in Cape Town, does he have the kind of political hold over communities that would guarantee the DA gets returned there for several more terms.

Only a racist fool or tactical idiot would therefore say, even in our race-obsessed country, that Wilmot is a better choice to lead the DA than Helen, just because he isn't white.

Don't get me wrong: he is bloody smart, and he has a solid academic and civil society career behind him to be proud of.

But the DA has to stop panicking about the race issue. Yes, a black leader is desirable, but the right one. Helen's qualities as a politician that make her a better sell to voters over Mamphela are the same qualities that make her a better sell over Wilmot. He is way too formal, lacks popular appeal when he speaks, and is like a wise uncle you want to consult in his study for advice worth taking really seriously. But he isn't the uncle who will deliver that cracking speech at your wedding, let alone MC the entire event. He just cannot stir a crowd and take a political message to the people. Helen is a better choice.

I say this to demonstrate two related points I am at pains to reinforce: (a) being a brilliant black person outside of politics doesn't mean you're the DA's answer to the racial headache; and (b) being a political brand that resonates with the electorate is necessary for effective leadership and it may be a quality that is in bigger supply in some white politicians than in some black politicians.

The DA should therefore be thoughtful in its search for a black leader. It should search in a manner that demonstrates a more sophisticated understanding of the kind of person who will resonate most strongly with the largest number of voters. The most important reason not to reopen the leadership negotiations with Mamphela, however, is the fact that she is too politically uncharismatic and stilted to do the job in a post-Zille DA.

Now, do not get me wrong. I am not suggesting you must be as flamboyant as US president Barack Obama. Look how many are now disappointed in him. And, of course, we need not take our cue from political contexts where bombast is rewarded.

However, Mamphela will not excel rhetorically and communicatively in our political arena. Just think of, say, the annual debate on the State of the Nation speech. There were brilliant speeches in 2013 from many, including most memorably and for different reasons, Mazibuko and Manamela.

Or, as another example, in the special parliamentary sitting that debated why our military men went to die in the Central African Republic, both the DA's David Maynier and Cope's Mosiuoa Lekota were brilliant. Their performances were templates of opposition accountability. Mamphela just does not have the pace, the debating agility, and the rhetorical flourish that goes with these varying parliamentary roles.

And, outside Parliament, she lacks these qualities too, as is already evidenced by a dwindling elections campaign.

The problem, however, with leaders like Lekota and Holomisa is that they have had their innings already in the parties that they have led, and as leaders they are spent political forces. While Madonna has been able to reinvent herself in the pop music world with every passing decade, it is very hard to project Lekota or Holomisa into a future over the next five to ten years in which they lead the DA to a victory or near-victory over the ANC. Their brands are tired.

* * *

Where does this leave the DA? Well, merging is unnecessary, and too risky for the reasons I have discussed. But welcoming as an ordinary member anyone into the party who is willing to accept the party's principles and processes is fine.

The party does need a black African leader in the post-Zille years, though. But Mamphela is not the right person to take over. In its anxiety to find a black African leader, it is important, as I have said, that the party remembers that while black is necessary, it isn't sufficient. And so it must have a very long and hard think about all the other qualities that a leader may or may not have.

In the end, I suspect, patience might be the name of the game. And the next party leadership contest may turn out to be one between Mazibuko and Maimane. Both had their careers inside the party effectively sponsored by Zille and there is much jealously about this, but in the next year or two it is worth keeping a very close eye on both of them to see if they can defy the weaknesses – real or imagined – that critics like myself have often highlighted in them.

But what the DA shouldn't do is to hastily merge with small parties or again offer the party to Ramphele. She just might say yes this time!

SO ... COULD I VOTE DA?

almost fell off my studio chair the other day. I was busy engaging my listeners while watching activity on Twitter. Because, you know, the modern man likes to multitask. And one of the items on my Twitter timeline was an article tweeted by Helen Zille. Being curious, I opened it, and to my utter surprise the very first sentence stated that she agreed with what one Eusebius McKaiser had written in the *Cape Times* that week.

The article she was referring to was my weekly column. In it I had argued that Helen had made a mistake by apologising for the way the DA had recently voted on a few pieces of legislation related to BEE. She had claimed that the party's parliamentary caucus had messed up, and that they had in good faith supported laws that they should in fact have scrutinised better, laws that are actually too draconian when it comes to how they try to get companies to change their demographic composition.

My point in the column was that, actually, Helen was simply scared of critics like Gareth van Onselen, and also others like

Tony Leon, Anthea Jeffery, John Kane-Berman, Frans Cronjé, etc. – all of whom had written columns, blogs or letters to newspapers bemoaning the DA having abandoned its liberal roots (supposedly) by supporting legislation that makes reference to racial categories. The DA, in their view, is meant to be non-racial, and by non-racial they mean not supporting policies that refer to blacks, whites, coloureds, etc.

This is, of course, utter rubbish. Non-racialism does not mean we do not, and should never, see groups in racial terms. It means something much simpler: not reducing someone to their race; and not behaving prejudicially on the basis of race. That's very different to pretending that racial categories are inherently poisonous, and denying that racial categories might ever be useful to us in the policy landscape.

And, as I explained in the first two chapters of this book, liberalism is often misunderstood by people who aren't really interested in political philosophy or ideology, but who are motivated by a desire to preserve power and privilege.

The bottom line is that there are many strands of liberalism. I had mentioned in that *Cape Times* column to which Helen referred that liberal egalitarianism, for example, is a version of liberalism that places deep value on substantive equality and, therefore, on social justice and redress.

There is nothing intrinsically illiberal about group identities, including racial categories. And so it was nonsense to accuse the DA of abandoning liberalism. These critics were simply not getting liberalism, or they were trying to define liberalism as colour-blindness, which is rather pathetic, since the history of liberalism in political thought is not littered with examples of thinkers and philosophers who see liberalism as necessarily implying that races and groups are invisible or non-existent.

And I said as much in that column, accusing the DA of being intellectually weak, in fact, in not pushing back against those critics who were making them feel guilty for supporting important laws aimed at redressing past injustices, laws that are not illiberal.

So, imagine my surprise to find Helen agreeing with me right upfront in her online newsletter that week. Actually, I was shocked. And the reason I was shocked is precisely because she is often so damn touchy, intransigent and tone deaf, as is the party more generally.

That afternoon I was having lunch with my publisher, ostensibly to celebrate the completion of this book. Over a fantastic piece of prime steak and a perfect wine pairing, our celebration turned to a question about the book, with me self-critically wondering whether we had, in fact, finished the project.

'Given the title we've chosen, Louise, I'm sure people will want to know ... *So, could I vote DA*? Maybe I should answer the question explicitly in the end?' The fact that we were having this discussion while also celebrating the book's apparent completion wasn't odd to us. But it might be for someone who came to the title literally – and I felt I had a duty to engage you as reader, as voter, in the terms I have framed the project.

I intended the book to discuss, as it has done, the range of issues that each of us grapple with as we think about the DA. But I cannot, as I mentioned at the outset, tell you who to vote for. That is your private political choice to make.

'Well, could you vote DA?' asked Louise.

The answer, actually, is one I am willing to reveal here, and Helen's newsletter that day was very relevant to explaining where I am at on the question this book poses in its title. Yes, I *could* vote DA.

I am not psychologically enslaved by the ANC. I am flexible in my political choices. In fact, I may or may not have voted DA before. Who knows?

This flexibility is not trivial, by the way. Many of my friends – political journalists and political analysts included – *could not* vote DA. They have told me this. It is not a live option for them. The DA stands no chance of persuading them; at best they can be engaged intellectually, but when they are in that voting queue, it will not even cross their minds to consider voting for the DA.

I think the *intensity* of the lack of openness to the DA is a shortcoming in my friends, though one that is rooted in their biographies, and not so much in the DA's biography. There is little the DA can do with this category of voter.

But voters like myself, who are still critical of the party, yet more open, are worth engaging, worth trying to persuade. But at times the party is just bloody lazy, conveniently pretending I might be like some of my friends who have an unshakable historical commitment to never, ever voting for the DA. That is a complacent, and false, assumption. The fact is: I *could* vote DA.

But, *will* I vote DA? Well, that depends on how the party deals with the concerns I have systematically laid out and discussed throughout the book. When I wake up, go to work, and find a newsletter that shows Helen is capable of not being intransigent, of hearing me out, and engaging me, then I think I should vote DA. Not because she agreed with my *Cape Times* article as such, but because she showed a willingness to actively listen, to consider criticism, and to partially reconsider her own position on issues of great importance: liberalism, race and redress.

Now that is a leader, and a party, worthy of my vote. For sure.

But, just as I was thinking, 'There goes my vote to the DA, guaranteed', I see news reports coming through of her saying that racial quotas are 'Verwoerdian', remarks she reportedly made at the Cape Town Press Club the same day she released the newsletter in which she agreed with my *Cape Times* column.

And then I sigh. (Insert HUUUUUGE sigh.) What the hell was Helen conceding then when she was 'agreeing' with one Eusebius? If she could relate to my column, then she could not be delivering a speech hours later in which she rejected the idea of racial quotas as morally and practically necessary and defensible in the service of redressing past injustices.

Simply put: she is one helluva confused party leader. And I

cannot vote for a party that doesn't know whether it is coming or going on a crucial issue like affirmative action in general, and BEE more specifically. And, related to these policy debates, I am tired of trying to puzzle through the confusion in the party's messaging on race in general – do they or do they not have a problem with the language of race? Do they accept that there are whites, blacks, coloured, etc? Or do they just see people with inner beauty and stuff?

And so, just as I think, yes, I will vote DA, I reign myself in, judging this party to be a hot mess, philosophically.

And so while I could vote DA, right now – as I type this coda – I will not do so because a policy question crucial to me as a voter is bungled by the party. However, a week is a long time in politics. I remain mightily unimpressed with the governance and leadership weaknesses of the ANC government. And if the DA gets its philosophical and policy houses in order between now and election day – and communicates with me in a way that isn't aggressive and annoying in tone – then I just may, actually, vote DA. My vote is up for grabs. All parties are welcome, though, to try their luck with me.